In Loving Memory of my Dearest Sister

Maria N. Sansiveri

The
ZERO-
SUM
GAME
— of —
YOU

Rosa L. Antonini

Published in the United States by KH Publishers..

ISBN	Hardcover	978-1-953237-60-6
ISBN	Paperback	978-1-953237-59-0
ISBN	eBook	978-1-953237-61-3

The Publisher does not have any control over and does not assume any responsibility for author or third-party websites or their content or any other media, social or other.

Printed in the United States of America

www.khpublishers.com

Cover design by Dezmond Carter
Book interior design by Davon Christian Brown

First Hardback Edition, December 2021

DEDICATION

I want to dedicate this book to the wonders of my world: Annabel and Dantez. Your arrival in my life opened the door of the most unconditional and profound love that I never imagined was possible to feel. Since your birth, you have become the number one priority in my Zero-Sum Game.

Annabel, my beautiful, loving, caring, and bright daughter, you brighten the day of everyone around you with your energetic and charming personality. Your hard-working habits and high-quality standards make a difference in anything you touch. After reading the first pages of one of my drafts, your words were, "I feel empowered." Those words meant the world to me because I know you can only say what you believe and feel.

Dantez, my wonderful son: Since you were a small child, you always showed how much you care for each one of us. A young man with few words but with a definite meaning. Your eyes are always full of kindness, warmth, and respect for others. The goodness of your heart makes you an extraordinary human being.

To my mother. To my husband. To my family. I love you always.

I also want to dedicate this book to YOU, the reader. Receive all my love. I believe in you.

ACKNOWLEDGMENTS

I must begin by thanking my incredible loving husband, Chris. From the first moment I told you about my idea for this book, you supported and believed in me without a single shred of doubt. You read my first draft with all my "Spanglish" mistakes and patiently listened to talks and endless ideas. During this process, you have been the perfect companion and have been an essential source of motivation, giving me your full support and the time I needed to write this book. I Love you! Thank you for your unconditional love for me and for the balance you bring to our family.

I want to thank my mother, Ana Alvarez, AKA Doña Tata, the person who made the most sacrifices to give me and my siblings an education, despite never getting one herself and regardless of financial constraints. You devoted your life to us. You are the living example that nothing can stop a person with intense desire in their hearts.

Thanks to my father, Juan Lopez (deceased), my brothers, El Negro(deceased), Juanito, Jose Miguel y Angel, my sisters Rosita(deceased), Ana, Josefa, Griselda, Maria(deceased). I couldn't ask for a better family. Each of you brings a different spice to the table, so we make this wonderful and unique Latino recipe together. You all mean so much to me. Love you always.

To Margaret Antonini, Donna Antonini, and Peter Antonini, for welcoming me into their families with an open heart. Thank you for your constant love, support, and presence for my family and me. Thank you for all your feedback and suggestions after reading my manuscript. I'm so lucky to have you in my life. Love you.

Words cannot express my gratitude and appreciation to Kia Harris from KH Publishers. I still remember our first phone call and its excitement as she listened to my over-excited tone of voice about my manuscript. You got excited as well. I felt your positive energy and your strong sense of helping first-time authors. You were instrumental throughout this process. You helped me overcome some of my obstacles to make this book a reality. You and staff, thank you so much for everything you did to convert my manuscript into this beautiful book.

I want to express my warmest thanks to my first editor, Emma Nnachi, Chief Editor at Fiverr. You used all your years of experience to perform the first set of edits of my manuscript. You were the first expert in the industry that believed in and loved my work. Thank you so much for being so supportive, Chief.

I want to thank my beautiful extended family, my wonderful friends, talented co-workers, and every person I have interacted with throughout my life. Without you, this book would not have come to life. I'm grateful to you.

Last but not least, to my dearest friend Simona, you bring motivation and determination everywhere you go. You draw out the best in every life you come across by transmitting the magic of light, harmony, and positivism. You helped me to break the shield that was preventing me from writing this book. My family and I are so lucky and grateful to have you in our lives. Thank you, and I love you always.

TABLE OF CONTENTS

ABSTRACT

In game theory, there is a concept known as a zero-sum game. A *zero-sum game* is a situation where one player's winnings are equal to another player's losses. As a result, the net change of the transaction is zero. A zero-sum game can have as few as two or millions of players, as in the currency trading market. At the end of a zero-sum game, there is no doubt about the winner or loser. There is no gray area. That's because the only way to win is by causing another person or group of people to lose.

What if I show you a different style of a zero-sum game? A game of life where you can always win without depriving someone else of something. A game where no one directly gains from your losses, and no one loses from your gains. A game where all other players are irrelevant, and the only one that counts is you. What if you could play this game on your own? What if I told you that you have already met all of the requirements needed to play? And more importantly, you have the power to win! Of course, as in any game, there are guidelines and defined rules. The nine guidelines here are written so that you understand your most probable outcome as a player of the game before investing time.

The main objective of *The Zero-Sum Game of You* is to focus on engaging activities related to your happiness and success. Despite the rules of the game, you are in charge of deciding how to play it at all times. As with any game, the more you play, the better you get. The net of your wins and losses define your outcome. You cannot blame anyone but yourself if you fail. Just like no one but you will claim the victory for winning.

Everything in the game depends on you. You define the targets and the strategy. You are the only player that matters in your zero-sum game. And regardless of your current mindset or situation, you have the necessary tools to play successfully.

Today, I invite you to play *The Zero-Sum Game of You.*

INTRODUCTION

In my late 20s, I became very interested in Foreign Exchange trading. It was amazing to see the daily fluctuations in the currency market. I would keenly study the charts at five o'clock in the morning, getting ready to place my trade before the market opened for business. Each currency market starts its business hours at a different time frame. From London, New York, Australia, and Tokyo, so there were plenty of options to play in the currency trading market at any time of day.

I took several courses and learned a collection of rules and guidelines about currency trading during this time. I was determined to learn and master the science of it. I traveled to Boca Raton, FL., to attend a boot camp on currency trading. After all my reading, research, studies, and applying all the theories, one thing became clear; from my perspective, currency trading was just another form of gambling. There was no real science behind it. There wasn't one rule that would give me a repetitive result for winning 100% of the time. Trading isn't based on skill or technique but rather the combination of different variables that, for the most part, are not accessible to regular individuals. During this process, I also learned that someone else was celebrating their winnings whenever I lost capital in my account. This was also true the other way around; every time I made some money, someone else lost their investment. This process is known as a zero-sum game. The net winnings equal the net losses, so the only way for someone to win is for another person to lose. Sounds a little evil, right? Well, if we enter the game, we must accept the rules. Similar rules apply to all sports played by two opponents; only one side can win.

This book is not about currency trading or any other type of trading. It's not about sports or gambling either. My objective in writing this book is to show how to use the zero-sum game rules as a means to improve your present situation and build a more fulfilling future. If you play the zero-sum game [of you], as presented in this book, I assure you; your life will be more fulfilling, have more purpose and enthusiasm than it currently has. You will become the most refined version of anything you want to be. The main objective of *The Zero-Sum Game of You* is, finding happiness, purpose, success, and unlimited gratitude without having regrets from your actions.

Gratitude is a commonly used word. However, many people use it but don't have the experience of living it. You can find this among people who use the word often yet still complain about vain things. Some people use the term to pray before eating and then spend the rest of the day or night criticizing others or lamenting events.

When we get to experience the real sense of gratitude, there is no turning back. The experience of gratitude changes our lives forever. We begin to view everything around us differently.

Once the feeling of gratitude surrounds us, we'll realize who we really are and what our purpose is. Gratitude makes us humble, and it enables us to experience emotions far beyond words. It is freedom and love. These feelings allow us to see outside the box and also remove all prejudice. Gratitude will enable us to understand the actions of others and their intended value. It helps us strengthen our sense of fairness, and it will keep our feet on the ground even after we conquer our most precious goals. Once we ignite the flame that starts the fire of gratitude, it keeps growing without effort; we will see it and feel it everywhere we go. We will realize there is no more need to seek happiness because we would have found it.

Gratitude is one of the rewards for playing this zero-sum game successfully. I strongly encourage you to give it a try and make it part of your goals. You will find a few options to play this game according to your desires. If you follow the guidelines, you will attain your goals, whatever they might be. I am not here to tell you what is best or worst for you; that is for you to decide. Allowing someone else to define what success means will make you an easy target to become a pawn in their game.

The objectives or targets we define for our game have to make sense to us. These goals should fill our souls with passion and happiness. The more we want something, the more motivation we will feel, translating into more effective actions towards our goals.

Have you ever seen two people playing a game of chess? What about tennis? If you are a fan of the sport, you most likely know the rules and will notice right away when one of the players makes a mistake. We all see actions differently depending on if we are a participant or a spectator. This is the main reason why *The Zero-Sum Game of You*, also represented as 0ΣU, is presented as a game. It enables you to see your past, present, and future moves from a different perspective.

I use the Sigma (Σ) symbol as a reminder that we are the sum of all of our parts. Within each of us exists a complex and enigmatic unique formula made of the attributes evident to the eye and what exists only in our conscious and subconscious minds. These extraordinary tangibles and intangible elements create this wonderful reality that enables us to be who we are and to have everything we need to become and achieve our intense desires that align with our inner being. There are many players and games all around us. The truth is, we are already part of a game. I intend to make you aware of it so that you may play effectively.

BACKGROUND

Since the beginning of time, human beings have managed to justify situations that have not resulted in pleasant outcomes. It is always easier to blame something or someone else for unwanted results. Invented excuses are prevalent in every environment where people interact, including immediate family, work, religious groups, politics, and society. The zero-sum game [of you] changes this approach by eliminating all external circumstances and every other person as the reason for your current state. It makes you confront your past and present by taking ownership of your actions and their outcomes. This new perspective will enable you to build a much more satisfying future.

When we witness a game between two people, we will likely judge the players' decisions differently than if we were playing the game. If we can see our life, as a game, including our past and present state of things, in a very objective way, we will be prepared to make better and more accurate decisions for our future. Why? Because this will remove our ego from our decision process, giving us much better chances to win our targets.

Many people work too hard for too long, only to realize they have wasted so much energy and effort for an unpleasant ending. This mismanagement of purposes usually happens when we are in a state of unawareness of our actions. We may be running too fast to notice we are running in a loop or pushing so hard we may fall off a cliff and be permanently unable to change direction.

At this point in life, you may be living your dream or be unhappy with your life. You may feel blessed, lucky, and prosperous, or perhaps you feel tired, unfortunate, and lack motivation. Those two states of being are easy to identify; they are like day and night. However, there is a third mindset; this is like the "gray area." There is a large group of people who fall within this third state of being. They lack a personal purpose in life. They don't know where they stand emotionally and mentally. They're neither satisfied nor dissatisfied with their lives. They just go whichever way the wind blows. They haven't spent the time to know themselves. In a way, they have adopted a way of living that protects them from the pain that can sometimes occur in life. They don't want to rock the boat or stir up any waters. They avoid trying too hard for fear of failing, and they have a constant desire to fit in. Because they lack core values, they begin to act like a chameleon. This mindset opens them up to continuous changes in their behavior. They try to fit according to the environment or the people around them.

The malleability that characterizes this group contributes to their loss of identity and character. Without self-acknowledgment of an inner purpose, a person can waste years pursuing targets that are not in line with who they are. *The Zero-Sum Game of You* (0ΣU) will help you objectively get to know yourself and better understand your strengths and weaknesses by utilizing self-awareness and motivation procedures while freeing you of limiting perceptions.

What we see around us and who we are is the outcome of all the battles we face in life. Within each of us, there are powers of diligence (leadership) vs. idleness (hopelessness). These competing forces face each other multiple times daily. Each time we decide or act one way or another, one of these tendencies wins while the other loses. With every step, we move toward an objective or away from it, and as a result, one of those forces is winning and recruiting more thoughts and emotions to ensure future winnings. A leader will tend to lead because, with every win, more memories and habits keep building, preparing them with more ammunition to win other tasks in the future.

An idle person who lacks authenticity will tend to follow others of a stronger will. Whenever our actions are not in line with our values or let others decide for us because of fear, this internal force keeps feeding on those fears. It will create more memories and habits to ensure that we keep driving in the wrong direction of living an unsatisfying life void of awareness and gratitude.

Due to a lack of authenticity, a follower will continue to follow and apply the force of least resistance either because of lack of self-esteem, accountability, or fear of failing. Whenever they do not control their actions, new memories and habits will continue being created and reinforced in the subconscious mind, making it harder to reach their full potential. Whenever our positive side loses a battle to our negative side, it reinforces behavior and emotions to help guarantee future losses. The same is true in the opposite direction.

Every time we accomplish something, every time we miss out on something, every time we act or behave passively, one of our internal forces is winning over the others. We can see the results of these combined wins and losses: rich people getting more prosperous, poor people getting poorer, happy people getting happier, and sad and angry people getting angrier and miserable. These internal forces work in teams. Each one of them feeds from specific types of thoughts and emotions. If an individual starts feeling angry for any reason, the inner source for this emotion keeps feeding on other similar beliefs and past experiences that triggered the same sentiment. The more this behavior is reinforced, the more it strengthens that person's weakness. Instead, if the person calms down and stops fueling anger, this new behavior will debilitate that weakness. From each battle between rage and composure, one of them will win. The one that wins will trigger the actions in line with that emotion. If anger wins, the person may hurt someone or commit an act that they may regret later. If calmness prevails, the person will take a constructive set of actions to deal with the situation. Daily, we all deal with different emotions that trigger actions in line with them. It is a continuous loop that you and I face each day. It is the constant battle of the zero-sum game of you.

Many psychologists classify human emotions into six categories: Happiness, Sadness, Anger, Surprise, Disgust, and Fear. As we can see, there are many more negative than positive emotions. Therefore, it is easier to fall prey and reinforce a negative pattern that works against us.

Playing the OΣU will expose each player to face their challenges and fears. The difference in winning won't depend as much on the things we have now or our current state of mind. Instead, it'll depend on the hunger we feel in our souls about becoming the best of our potential. We are not robots. Our mind is an incredible tool, and if we utilize it effectively, it will give us the power to control about 95% of all situations we need to deal with in life. Also, it will help ease the emotions and their durations, as created by the other 5%. It is typical to experience situations that drag us down, and it is OK to feel bad for a moment. It is OK to cry and feel miserable for a bit, but always recognize it as a phase, a period that, no matter how hard it feels at the moment, it will pass. It is entirely reasonable to have bad days; however, learning the cycle of thoughts, emotions, and actions prepares us to win in our OΣU.

The more we generate a thought, the stronger we build the habit to auto-generate more images of the same thought process in the future. The faster we can interrupt the loop of negative thoughts created by one detrimental idea, the better equipped we become for future challenges. The current situation of our life and relationships with our family, friends, coworkers, and others are, in significant part, the outcome of our thinking process and emotions. So, if emotions have the power to make us feel happy or miserable, why are so many people unhappy and unsatisfied? Why not choose to be in the best and more constructive state of mind that we can be?

In this book, you will learn how to bring your positive

internal forces into the zero-sum game [of you]. These forces are part of your daily life, and they independently influence your every decision. The stronger mindset conquers the weaker attitude each time. The number of wins and failures will determine what your future unfolds. Either positivity will win, or negativity will win. You get to decide. If your predominant force is not bringing you happiness, don't despair. I will give you tools that'll help you build a happier life.

We all have friends or family who are go-getters and others known to be more laid back, always making the slightest effort to succeed. Sometimes it is easier to judge others than it is to judge ourselves. The person considered a couch-potato and the one thought a go-getter has a constant winning force. This translates into a series of habits that ensures more wins or losses of battles in their future. The warrior force within the go-getter will continue growing and getting stronger to ensure more successes, just as the hopeless force within the slacker will continue building more negative habits to ensure its victory as well.

If you think this is not real and don't feel these inner powers, more likely, one of your forces has taken over the other completely, to the point, you don't feel it anymore. This unawareness can happen intentionally or unintentionally. The stronger one side gets, the more habits you will form in that direction. The longer you reinforce these habits, the harder and longer it will take to replace them. The good news is, with determination, you can always change to what you want to be.

Once you begin playing the zero-sum game [of you], you

will perceive life a little differently. You will notice that other players around you are playing their own game, purposefully or by default. As your level of awareness increases and you learn to manage your thoughts further, everything else but your game will become noise. The more you accept your level of accountability, the higher feeling of freedom you will experience. The more you practice being in control of your game, the more you will see that everything that happens to you is primarily because of you.

There will be uncontrollable and unpredictable events in life for which we have no control. However, you fully control your reactions to such events. There are losses that only time can heal. The way you live, the things you do, the level of gratitude, and a sense of awareness will ensure that you won't have any regrets and won't want to change the past if such happens to you. Life is constantly moving, and unexpected events may occur at any point. Living your life with full awareness enables you to appreciate the big and the small and perceive emotions that could go unnoticed otherwise.

The OΣU does not judge the type of goal each player decides to pursue. The game does not care about the fairness or unfairness of the target. There have been influential (known and unknown) leaders in history who used their OΣU for positive and harmful endeavors. For example, a notorious drug dealer may have had a goal to sell the most drugs and obtain the most significant number of clients possible, creating a self-focused win, with each client being a pawn in their game.

People lacking mental and emotional strength tend to live by default, meaning without a purpose or goals. Thus, by lacking specific goals and living under a state of unawareness and self-pity, they become a perfect target to be a pawn in someone else's game. If everyone took control over their own game, making their own choices according to their goals and plan of action, there would be less power for abusive and self-centered people like drug dealers, dictators, manipulators, oppressors, and malicious master-minds. As we can see, a person can learn, master the game and use it to exploit the power and take advantage of others, but it is up to us not to allow anyone to take advantage of us.

In the 0ΣU, some people define a goal to increase their financial assets, while others seek to conquer other goals that bring them happiness. Happiness for some can be to obtain a college education or to complete a business project, as examples. You can choose any target that motivates you. But to win the game, the most important thing is, you must achieve your objectives without [or minimal] regrets over your actions. Before you start playing, it's important to get complete awareness of your current state of being and your desired ultimate state of being because there is no do-over.

Achieving your goals without regrets is the number one rule for winning the game. You may be wondering, "What do I do about my previous regrets?" The first thing is to know that you are not alone. We all have something we are not proud of. But the past is already written. You have the power to decide if you will let go and define who you are now and who you will be. You can choose to learn from the past and use those lessons to ensure that your present and future align with the person you want to be. If you feel like you need to take some actions to make peace with your past, go ahead and do it so you can move on. Nothing positive will happen if you continue dueling with the past. History cannot be rewritten. Playing this game at your command will enable you to be constantly aware of your present, so you can begin building your future the way you want.

Before setting up the strategy for your OΣU, you will need to determine your current state of mind and the conditions affecting your daily life. These conditions may be tangible and intangible things that are part of you and your surroundings. This identification will include the things that are important to you and the things that influence you. It does not matter if these factors are considered negative or positive. If you miss some elements on your first draft, you can always come back to adjust your baseline. I assure you that you have all you need to start playing this exciting game and succeed, independent of where you are right now. Once the identification process is complete, you will be ready to start setting up your targets. Your life will become much more relaxed and fulfilled once you begin playing [to win] and start seeing some results.

INFLUENCE OF CULTURE AND BELIEFS ON YOUR GAME

Since we were born, our parents, grandparents, and ancestors' cultural traits and beliefs have been abundant in our immediate environment. Social, political, educational, and religious heritage factors influence our core values. All of these elements mold our lives as we grow. They affect the lens through which we perceive our realities, morals, and values.

We often see our culture and beliefs as permission to behave and judge others according to our standards. Often, in many cases, we don't take the time to question whether our ancestors' norms have the same relevance in our era and whether they should be passed on to future generations. Understanding the roots that have formed our habits and society is one of the first activities we will engage in to get our minds into a clean state free of prejudice and fear.

The Zero-Sum Game of You will empower you to take charge of your life. It will awaken new desires and interests unique in value to you. If you stick to it, it will open your eyes to better realities about people, skills, jobs, society, and your role in finding happiness. It will enable you to bridge the gap between where you are and where you could be. You may experience some discomfort in the initial phase. For some, it will mean facing some realities within yourselves, confronting past actions and pains so that you can heal.

Our perspective of life changes as we get older. Time and experiences create strong bonds between our beliefs about ourselves, our minds, and subconscious minds. At every age, we have certain advantages. As a young adult, you can use the OΣU to make crucial decisions that will provide shortcuts that will prevent you from unnecessary pain and frustration in the future. If you are older, embracing this game will help you brighten your present and future by taking ownership of your past and learning to live your life to the fullest, based on what you want, without resentment, regret, or sadness. Your energy sources never age. If you feel motivated to set new goals, your energy sources will be rejuvenated. When you get stuck and think there is nothing else you can obtain or achieve, you will begin to die internally. Your body will continue moving and breathing, but you become a rudderless shipwreck if you have no interest in anything new or different.

If you find yourself without any interest in pursuing something, you can focus on doing something for someone else. Engaging in any activities where you concentrate on another person or animal's needs will trigger sentiments of purpose. When you focus on helping someone else without any expectations, your lives will find meaning and ignite a fire in your hearts to keep you going and enjoying your journey. For some, the gift of giving comes naturally. For others, it is an entirely new gesture and will require conscious effort. If you are part of this second group, I highly encourage you to try. I assure you, it will be one of your best decisions, as it will bring you more happiness and joy.

It may be easier for younger people to change their beliefs because their associations and results are not ingrained in their subconscious, typically through many years of reinforcements. Understanding the role of our cultures' principles and root causes allows us to decide how much we want our culture to continue influencing the way we make current and future choices. Respecting a culture does not mean accepting it without question, especially if it can hurt us or others. One of the first exercises the OΣU suggests is questioning everything, including those habits and traditions we learned by default. Understanding helps build ownership.

A beautiful friend of mine, Doris Cummings, told me about a cooking recipe her grandma used to make for family gatherings. One of the main requirements of this recipe involved mixing and then cooking all ingredients in a tiny pot. She grew up enjoying this tradition, just like the rest of her family. After she got married, she continued with the practice. However, she found it challenging to prepare the meal for many people due to the pot size restriction which the recipe called for. One day, she ignored that aspect of the recipe and prepared the same formula in a larger pan. To her surprise, the flavor was the same. She explained that she initially felt a little guilty about changing the recipe until she realized that this tradition started centuries ago when the country struggled financially. Her grandmother cooked this recipe in a small pot because it was the only size she could afford. Many times we all do things because that is the way we've learned or the way we've seen it done. Suppose we maintain a curious mind and keep asking ourselves the reason behind our thinking process and actions. In that case, we will build a sense of accountability and ownership of everything we do.

Let me give you another example. I grew up washing my underclothing every time I took a shower. It was a cultural habit. I was judgmental of people who did not do the same thing. As I got older, I continued this practice in auto mode. This activity was a mandatory task that I needed to do every day, even while on vacation. I even tried to force this habit on my daughter when she was little. One day, after listening to the small pot recipe story, I realized that there was no need for me to continue carrying this tradition either. Even though this tradition is practiced regularly in my culture of origin, the roots do not indicate excellent hygiene, as I thought. However, this cultural habit started because there was a lack of underclothing due to financial limitations. The only way to keep one clean underwear daily was by washing the used one while showering. I have to admit; I still practice this tradition as a matter of habit; however, I no longer feel the pressure of obligation, nor do I judge others who don't do it.

Grasping the root of habits eliminates prejudice toward people who don't engage or believe in the same activity. Without understanding its origin and questioning its effectiveness in our current setting, we can continue exercising, passing on, and enforcing unnecessary habits on future generations. Considering the origins of everything we do and believe creates a sense of awareness and ownership of our actions. Mainly because sometimes these beliefs are not harmless like the ones we just discussed. We need to pay special attention to cultural beliefs that can influence us to harm others or ourselves. Does it make sense to continue supporting an enmity that started centuries ago with root causes that are irrelevant today? Does it make sense to harm someone else just because it is part of our culture's religious inclinations or other beliefs?

Some people see their religion as the only worthy religion. Some also feel the same way about other convictions. Many people are non-believers in any religious practice or atheists. Within this group, there are different perspectives about what a religion is. For example, some atheists consider that religion is used as a means of social control. In a conversation with attorney Jose Miguel Lopez, he described how he believes religions play a role in maintaining a balanced society. He stressed that the media, religious practices, law enforcement, criminal law, and thus everything intended to serve a state so that each community and citizens can live together in balance are means of social control. "I consider and am convinced that this is the case because of my condition as a non-believer and atheist. I understand that if we manage to get a person to behave in a predetermined way by their own will, whoever establishes this regimen or conviction is winning. Suppose a person is a genuine follower of any religion and follows all rules and principles of it. In that case, they will need to behave according to those rules to receive the kingdom of their heaven; hence this minimizes the need to repress unwanted behaviors."

As we can see, there are many views respective to religious beliefs and the lack of them. If we all maintain an open mind while understanding our beliefs and respecting others' beliefs, we can make more informed decisions based on our awareness and principles. In addition, this will help us to recognize when others are trying to brainwash us.

Having a solid perception of righteousness can trigger a feeling of superiority and a wrong perspective to judge, manipulate and hurt others that don't see things the way we do. We all have the social responsibility to respect each other's origins, religions, and races. When a person does something under the influence of culture and beliefs does not change the facts. When all is said and done, that person alone will answer for all of their actions.

ASSESSMENT OF YOUR HABITS

Take a piece of paper or electronic device and write a short statement that describes some of the most common things you do just because it is part of your culture. This list should include things you and your family do with or without a specific reason based on inherited beliefs or practices. Keep an open mind; think about your religious beliefs, political preferences, and social perspective. Please include what you think about race, financial status, gender or sexual orientation, and love. Remember, this is a conversation with yourself only, so be as candid as you can be. Please take a few seconds to look at each of them; pay attention to the feeling that each one brings to you.

Now, ask yourself these questions about each one of the habits and philosophies you just identified.

- Why do I maintain this conviction?
- What motivates me to think this way?
- Do my feelings or thoughts come from freedom or fear?
- Do I feel happy when I act on my beliefs?
- Is this in line with my core priorities and goals?

- Would I be proud and without regrets on my deathbed?
- What reasons do I have to pass these beliefs on to my descendants?
- Does this habit, belief, or culture cause me to harm myself or someone else?

The definition of "harm" from the Oxford dictionary states, "harm is defined as physical injury, especially that which is deliberately inflicted: injury, hurt, pain, suffering, distress, anguish, trauma, torment, grief, damage, impairment, destruction, loss, ruin, defacement, defilement, mischief." It is essential to know the universal definition of harm because, for some, inflicting pain on others might not be seen as a damaging activity because of their beliefs.

Now that you have a clearer understanding of the meaning of harm, answer this question again. Do I practice actions that are the product of a habit or cultural belief that can cause me to harm myself or someone else mentally or physically?

It takes time and effort to change a habit. To change a pattern, you will need to get to the root source so your mind can gain clarity and awareness of all the elements that created it. Changing habits and thoughts ingrained in your mind your whole life is more challenging than changing or gaining newer ones. Nevertheless, it is essential to understand what you think, say, and do regularly to gain ownership of your life. Having ownership of your 360-degree environment is the motivation you need to be proud of yourself. Also, it'll provide the limitless potential to undertake whatever you want.

One story I heard many times as a child and young adult is "the camel and the needle." The moral of the story is, "It is easier for a camel to pass through the eye of a needle than for a rich man to enter the kingdom of God." Growing up, I knew many people who would label any wealthy person as "evil" because of their wealth. Many individuals who felt this way weren't pursuing a better financial life for their sake or their loved ones. They had a spiritual belief that their higher power wouldn't be happy with them if they pursued wealth. They had a fundamental pride in living in constant hardship.

I am not a theologian, nor am I pro or con of any religion. For some, religion is a source of hope, while for others, it is a source to help to manage or control societies. Independent of all subjective beliefs, each religion imbibes the principle of having a God or Gods or some other supernatural figures who are perfect, with an absolute source of pure energy, light, and love. I find it interesting that despite having these beliefs as a core foundation, there has been so much death, throughout history, in the name of a God or a religious belief.

If you are a parent, you'll understand that parents love their children. Any healthy relationship between parents and children requires a balance of love and discipline. In most cultures, if one child isn't behaving, a parent does not approach the "good" child and asks them to discipline harm, or worst of all, kill the lousy child (children) in the name of religion. The point is if someone proclaims to be a child of a higher power and people who practices the same beliefs are their "sisters and brothers," they are not inclined or instructed through their beliefs to discipline those who are not practicing the rituals perfectly. So, a "God" that is perfect will never push for violent vengeance towards any part of society.

As you tread the path of playing the OΣU, be sure to question each of your beliefs with an open mind and search for knowledge about root causes and implications. This way, you can free yourself from damaging views and concentrate on building a better present and fulfilling future.

I believe that those born wealthy and those impoverished deal with different challenges in their journeys, but both have the necessary tools to improve their lives. There is no point in blaming the past for your present and building more of the same perception by continuously seeing yourself as a victim.

While in college, one of my classmates always complained about how hard it was for her to go to school while working two jobs to pay for it. Though she loved her family, she could not overcome the mindset that life was unfair, where the rich had everything while others had nothing. Even though she eventually became a professional and moved to a better, bigger house, in her mind, she continued to see herself as a victim.

A few years later, while working for one of the largest financial institutions in New York, I met a great friend. Her upbringing was a little different than the friend I met at college. She was born into a very wealthy home in one of the prime areas of Manhattan. She grew up with everything and anything that money could buy. Yet, she struggled with depression. She spent most of her childhood and teen years with nannies. She also spent a lot of time alone since both of her parents had very demanding jobs. She became the victim of her situation.

Both of these individuals are great human beings, and both have dealt with different sets of challenges. Both realities are equally memorable. And while they are both unique, they ended up with similar outlooks on life. Just like our experiences are unique to us, considering that one person should be happier because of more financial resources can be wildly inaccurate.

Our perceptions are subjective to what we see within ourselves, which means it is like thinking that the truth is what we see through our custom lenses instead of opening our minds, taking our lenses off, and accepting others without judging. Comparing ourselves to another or complaining about our situation compared to someone else's shouldn't be a practice we indulge in. The only person who matters in the OΣU is you. That makes you 100% accountable for your present and future.

A complaint reinforces a negative thought. This, in turn, triggers a chain of more unconstructive thoughts, which then become negative emotions. If you start your day with unfavorable emotions, you won't perform at your highest capacity. If you don't put 100% energy and effort into everything you do, you will become accustomed to living an average life. The more complaints and negative thoughts you entertain, the more undesirable emotions you will experience. No one can build a better future while feeling like a victim of something or someone. If you consider yourself a victim or unlucky, you need to use the energy from within to flip your game, so you'll start moving in a different direction. Start by making peace with your past. After all, there is nothing you can do about it. What's done is done, and whatsoever happened is irrelevant now.

If you need to make amendments, then you need to act right now. If some relationships are broken and are worth repairing, then go ahead and start the process. Your future is in the making at this precise moment. Today you can use the lessons learned to your advantage. Taking some time to get within yourself is essential to understand your thinking process's roots and beliefs. One method I find helpful in this process is to create a checklist with all your views. Then think about all you know about the way you view things. Next, make a conscious decision about which perspectives you will keep and which you'll discard. By the end of this exercise, you should feel proud of the beliefs you have decided worth holding, and more importantly, you should feel that you own them.

Today is the past of your tomorrow. Today is the most valuable resource you have because it allows us to be and enjoy this moment. We can celebrate who we are and build the future that fits our desired reality.

THE POWER OF YOUR THOUGHTS AND EMOTIONS OVER YOUR GAME

Thoughts are a crucial part of your journey, and they are one of your most valuable assets. They possess the magic touch that determines if you'll win or lose the OΣU. Thoughts have the power to lift you or bring you down. They are seeds that, when planted correctly, will flourish into amazing tangible things. However, they can mess up your life with many unnecessary complications when ignored or planted on bad soil. Many influential people in the world have learned how to manage their thoughts and use them to their advantage.

The power of your thoughts is one of humanity's greatest gifts, but many take it for granted. If you leave your thoughts unattended, they can do you more harm than your worst enemy. Uncontrollable thoughts are like having a hundred children running around, jumping, and doing all sorts of things to catch your attention. Any situation can activate one of them, and then, all of a sudden, dozens more join the party, putting your life in a continuous state of stress and anxiety. The great news is you have power over your thoughts. However, this fantastic ability loses its constructive value and potential if you don't use, nurture, or care for it.

The mind, when unattended, is prone to become dominated by a particular line of thoughts. Let's do a quick-thinking exercise. This exercise will give you the baseline for your lines of thought. Do this before playing the OΣU, so you can compare your new way of thinking with the results of this exercise after successfully winning one round of the game.

Start by either closing your eyes or focusing on one single point on the wall. Try not to think about anything at first. You will notice that thoughts will automatically begin filling up your mind. Once this process begins, let your mind wander for 2-3 minutes.

What came to your mind? Did you have thoughts about people or things? Were your thoughts about things you like or dislike? Did your thoughts present worries or concerns about your job, kids, parents, and or partners? What specific emotions are you experiencing right now? Did these thoughts trigger feelings of happiness or sadness? Motivation or frustration? Do you feel relaxed or stressed out?

While doing this exercise, you may notice that many thoughts will come to your mind. Know that all thoughts don't have the same level of importance. The ones you need to pay attention to are those that generate emotions within you. A single thought, by itself, is not as relevant as the feelings and state of mind it triggers.

Let's imagine that a person had a disagreement with a colleague, friend, or family member. At the time of the argument, there was a video camera that recorded the whole event. In the recording, you can hear the following words, "You are a selfish, self-centered person who just thinks about yourself." We know based on the recording that those words are the facts. There is no doubt about it; we can hear it word by word in the recording. Now let's go over the process of emotions and how they affect the person according to their mindset. If the person has an anger mindset, then the arguments explained above will trigger negative emotions. These comments will generate feelings of anger, making them believe that the other person is ungrateful, not worthy, a hypocrite, etc. With every thought within the same emotion frequency, more anger and rage will get generated. If, instead, the person has a constructive mindset, they will hear the same exact words, but the emotions triggered will be completely different. Those words may be a call for attention or a cry for help. This second mindset understands that not everyone knows how to canalize their emotions more constructively.

As you can see, from this example, how you manage your thoughts can change your emotional state of mind. In this scenario, we can see how the perception and understanding of the same words generated anger and disgust under a non-constructive mindset while rendering compassion and empathy under a constructive mindset.

If there is one thing you can engage in and see results

right away, it is trying to understand how thoughts and emotions feed themselves to the point you act or react with a related set of actions. An action can build or destroy someone. Our thoughts and emotions fuel our actions. The thoughts in our minds are the root for everything we will become, so lay special attention to the type of thoughts you allow in your mind. Our thoughts are the seeds that we plant in our souls. If we select the right seeds and nurture them every day, we will get fruitful outcomes to achieve and become everything we want.

Thoughts ➤ Emotions ➤ Actions is the repetitive cycle that, in a way, molds our personalities and the way we act or react to our daily routines. Trying to control our thoughts is like trying to hold water with our hands. Just as water slides through our fingers without much notice, thoughts will appear in our minds without our consent. However, if we learn to interject a chain of negative thoughts with more constructive ones, we will be able to change the feelings we experience, resulting in our state of mind. The objective here is not to concentrate on controlling all thoughts; that would be impossible. The free flow of thoughts is the seed for new ideas and creativity. So, we don't seek to suppress this unique resource; instead, I will show you how to train the thinking process so that it is more effective in helping you achieve whatever you want.

Once you become the boss of your thoughts, you will minimize the stress and frustration you encounter daily. A clear and steady mind can help you make better decisions. Many health benefits have been associated with a quiet mind--from reducing stress and anxiety to reducing inflammation and mitigating diseases. The OΣU will guide you through some exercises on how to silence your mind anytime you wish. These techniques come especially handy when you need to stop yourself from reacting negatively or when you need to stop a chain of thoughts that are taking you in the wrong direction.

THINKING PROCESS VS. SOFTWARE ENGINEERING

One of my work specialties is designing and building computer software. I am fascinated by some of the things we can do within software engineering, specifically with data. Over the years, I realized our thinking process and emotions behave very similarly to computer software. There are some basic computer games where users are asked to enter an answer to a determined question. Once a user enters a response, the software provides feedback, such as a smiley face if the answer is correct or a sad face if the answer is wrong. Pre-written code controls this feedback. This code uses some logic with predetermined criteria to make the software or game behave one way or another as it responds to various inputs. A software developer could easily change the code and make the program behave differently.

Nonetheless, once the coding is in place, it does not matter which user or how many users play the game; it will always provide the same answer to the same type of inputs. The written code does not care, nor does it understand the meaning of a happy or sad face. The software code has no feelings, and it does not ask why we are making it behave one way or another; it just performs in auto mode.

During the design phase of any software, we can control and adjust the logic the way we want. The software engineer has total autonomy to decide what the primary purpose of the software is and to write the code any way they want, as long as it accomplishes the ultimate objective of the product. Once this software is in production, it becomes more complicated to make changes, even if necessary, to improve a feature. If we write the code correctly, we will not need any modifications once it is deployed. It becomes a repetitive mechanism that works in auto mode. Now anyone can run the program without the software developer's assistance. Like computer software, our thinking process starts with one thought or an idea in our mind. Then right after, a chain reaction starts, and more similar views join. Causing our reaction to a specific thought to be on auto mode each time the input (thought) comes to mind. However, one main difference between computer software and our thinking process is; a computer has no feelings. In contrast, and thankfully, our thoughts trigger a sound set of emotions that leads us to exhibit particular behaviors, first with ourselves and then around others. In other words, we have feelings.

Thoughts alone don't cause harm, but the emotions that come with them can steer our lives in a specific direction. Repetitive thoughts keep building repetitive and deeper similar feelings. These emotions drive the way we behave and the actions we take. These emotions will get us closer or further away from our goals. If we start our day with one negative thought and do nothing to correct its course, we will end our day with a very unsatisfactory outcome. Our minds and emotions have been preprogrammed to react in a specific way. Each person has a distinct form of responding to certain situations. We have a unique way of thinking, influenced by our social environment, parents, friends, culture, beliefs, and personal learning experiences. This unique thinking process and the resulting emotions it manifests started building in our brain [code] since we were a child. By now, many of the thoughts and feelings we feel are part of our brain software that runs in auto-mode. Most are due to the force of habit. They have become instructions to our subconscious mind.

The more a repetitive behavior is reinforced, the more fixed it becomes, thus turning it into a habit. According to different studies, a person can build a habit by doing something consecutively for an average of sixty-six (66) days. Many people believe that twenty-one days is enough to create a practice, but I have tested this theory on myself and concluded that twenty-one days is not enough. After twenty-one days, we would have developed the memory of the habit we are trying to create, but our mind and body will not perform it in auto mode. After twenty-one days, I found myself making an effort to accomplish the activity instead of an automatic reaction.

According to other studies, depending on the habit's simplicity or complexity, it could take anywhere between 18 to 254 days to build a new habit or get rid of an old one. Once we create a habit, our reactions become automatic. Our subconscious mind does not question the instructions we give it, whether right or wrong. It will perform our demands based on the way we have "written our code." We write a new code every day when a specific set of thoughts get into our minds. The subconscious mind does not react as much to our thoughts as to the emotions triggered by them.

You can waste more time making excuses and blaming others for your negative behaviors, lack of opportunities, and social disparities, or you can accept responsibility and take ownership of your conduct and actions. This is your first step to growth and freedom. You are the sole software engineer in your life. Up to this point, your internal code has been unconsciously written by your or others' influence. However, it is time to take complete control and write it to fit your goals. This is your game, and you are in control of the rules and strategy. Remember, there is no one else to blame. Your life, perceptions, actions, and the outcome are your full responsibility.

I have known individuals brought up in entirely dysfunctional families, exposed to drugs and alcohol from their early years. However, these same individuals still became professionals who have never consumed alcohol or drugs, with stable jobs and exemplary families. In contrast, others faced with the same circumstances continuously allow themselves to feel like victims. The significant difference between these two outcomes is how the person manages and disciplines their thoughts and actions.

Thoughts are like a spiral or set of dominos; once one shows up, it triggers a chain reaction, and more of the same begins flowing to our mind. Thoughts alone aren't much of a concern, but the feeling they bring can make much difference. Once a chain of thoughts starts in our mind, each thought brings a little more emotion than the prior one. This can work to our advantage; it can bring about feelings of satisfaction and happiness that deepen even more with each thought chain. Then again, it can work against us. In this case, we will end up sad, upset, angry, dissatisfied, and any other synonym for a state of perpetual unhappiness. Managing our thoughts is a necessary tool to learn. Learning to use them properly is one of the practices you will exercise in your OΣU.

Your thoughts and perceptions are a crucial part of your success. When you are unaware of them, they can drive you toward a path full of complications and confusion. I want to emphasize the word "unaware." When you are unaware of what's causing your decisions and actions, you become vulnerable for others to take advantage of you. The drug market, dictators, manipulators, sects, gangs, and abusive human beings take advantage of most individuals who are living in a constant state of unawareness and those who live believing they're victims.

The way you think today contributes to building what your future brings. Every thought adds to this process. A fresh set of ideas brings emotions that motivate you to take actions that bring more similar experiences. This indefinite loop activates either a constructive or destructive response. The only way to break the destructive loop is by introducing a new pattern of thoughts to engineer a new course of action.

Some people feel hopeless because their life seems to be a sequence of the same events. Many times, they consider themselves unlucky and a victim of society; for thousands of reasons. The reality is, even for those that feel paralyzed, they are within a loop as well. They keep dwelling on the same line of thoughts, which brings the same kind of emotions—as a result, generating similar unwanted tangibles that create another set of complaints and negative thoughts that starts the loop all over again. If unrewarding results continue, you need to break your existing thought patterns.

OVERRIDING YOUR THOUGHTS & EMOTIONS SOFTWARE

If you feel happy, fulfilled, and grateful for your life and the relationships you have, then keep doing what you're doing. But, if you tend to feel sad or angry, if you are struggling to accomplish some of your goals, if you feel an empty space within you with or without reason, or if there is anything about your life that you would like to change, then this section is for you.

The first step in playing the OΣU is defining your goals, which I will elaborate on later. But before you start making your list of goals, it is essential to clear your mind of prejudice and negative beliefs; otherwise, they'll affect your plans.

Your current state of things, including your job, relationships, financial status, and perception of life, is very connected to the emotions you feel in your daily routine. These emotions are triggered by your thoughts and the influence of your inner circle. You need to shift your desired emotions to your current situation. What does this mean? It means to learn to appreciate what you have now, not what you want to do, want to have, and want to be. You need to identify at least one thing that you love and feel grateful for now. Being able to acknowledge and find pleasure in the little things generates a set of positive and constructive emotions that will change your perspective of the events around you. This does not mean you should negate reality and try to live in a fictitious bubble. If you need to take a test and don't study for it, it doesn't matter how many times you repeat, "I will pass the test," the fact is, unless you put in some effort and study the material, you most likely will fail the test.

Being grateful for your current state of affairs isn't an encouragement to become lazy and comfortable to the point you become passive and monotonous. The fact that you are reading this book is evidence that you are curious and eager to explore ways to improve your life. This is a quality for which you can be happy. Many people don't dedicate time to acquiring knowledge that could help them eliminate the obstacles in their life. You know your circumstances, so you need to recognize anything you can use as a resource now. There is no magic. The grass might seem greener on the other side, and sometimes it is, but that should not take your spirit away. Instead, that should motivate you to achieve your goal if it's what your heart desires.

When people are happy and satisfied with who they are and what they do, they want to see everyone happy. You can use this quality to measure if you've reached the state of living in gratitude. When you come to this state, you will bless your friends and neighbors for their success. You will help them achieve what they want if it is in your power to do so.

Gratitude and happiness are such that the more we experience it, the more well-being we want for everyone, regardless of the color of their skin, race, education, or financial status. Gratitude enables us to see the real version of everyone, and it grants us the opportunity to experience love and kindness from all beings around us. The most important reason to feel gratitude for the things we have and the things we can do right now is that it raises our energy and vibration level, and it feels good experiencing the feeling that comes with it. Our brains love to do things that continuously please us. So it will give us more to feel grateful about.

The positive energy, synergy, vibration, and emotions will generate more of the same feelings. This positive and constructive chain reaction will empower you to accomplish your most desired goals more quickly. Once you get your mind in a state of gratitude, it will trigger positive emotions within yourself. At this point, it's time to draw thoughts and images related to the things you want in your life. I like to call this process "reusability of emotions." The more natural these new thoughts and feelings engulf your mind and body, the more creative and resourceful you become. This new mindset will open opportunities of making your dreams a reality, which you did not see before, to make our dreams a reality. Learning and practicing the art of managing your thoughts and emotions will exponentially improve the odds of achieving your goals while enjoying the journey.

OVERRIDING EMOTIONS EXERCISE

The concept of overriding emotions was introduced to me by a psychology graduate student who tried to help me overcome a panic attack while commuting through a tunnel. He urged me to think of multiplication or division operations. According to his studies, the objective of performing mathematical operations is to absorb the brain in the task entirely, so it stops fueling anxiety. The moment another thought takes over our full attention, the emotions originated by the first trigger will start to dissipate.

If you want to break a feeling of anger, you must stop thinking about the source of the event that got you angry. Please don't give in to the temptation to call that nosy friend, who you know will only add more fuel to the fire. Another thing to avoid is calling or facing the person you are irritated with at the moment. This can result in further disagreement and miscommunication. The best thing you can do is talk to or face this person after getting your mind into a different state. Once you are calm, you would have successfully lowered your anger and be able to implement a constructive course of action at that point.

The only way to avoid regrets is by taking actions or making decisions while in a stable, centered state of mind. We always want to act in a self-controlled manner rather than react out of anger. Remember, one of the rules of the OΣU is, you are accountable for everything you do. All your outcomes, good and bad, successes and failures, will reflect which part of you is winning your internal battles. Additionally, to succeed, you need to be sure or at least trust that you will not regret your actions. The reality is that you start and end a cycle every day. With every step forward, you can change your course and create a new approach. But this does not replace what has taken place in your yesterday. No one gets to go back in history for a do-over.

The first step to override an emotion is to break the chain of thoughts that generate unwanted feelings. You can do this by simply focusing your minds on another image, situation, or outcome. In the beginning, you can utilize an engaging book, TV show, or even the news. If you don't have anything around you, you can block your emotions by trying the math problem technique I explained above. Choose a challenging math problem so your mind can't get the answer right away; this will flip your attention and break the negative chain of thoughts.

WE NEED ENERGY TO WIN THE OΣU

SIX SOURCES OF ENERGY AND MOTIVATION

"Be positive" is a phrase we often hear and use in challenging situations. What does the expression "be positive" mean to you? How can you generate positive and constructive feelings when you are going through difficult circumstances?

Some people suggest the repetition of positive statements helps us feel better when experiencing an unfortunate event. I have found that telling yourself things like, "I feel happy," "Everything is good now," or "I feel great," while experiencing an overwhelming, painful or depressing condition can cause more harm than good. In addition to dealing with the negative feelings you are experiencing, saying these phrases will feel like you're lying to yourself. Therefore, it will add further negative emotions to the ones we already have. Chanting words or phrases opposite to your current emotions won't put you in a positive state. So how can you help yourself in those situations?

The first thing I find very helpful is to identify the root cause of the sentiment. Then, it is crucial to dispassionately understand if the issue can be resolved or if it needs to be let go. If there is a solution to the problem, then take the first step. Every action generates energy that boosts your creative mind power. Finally, find something to smile about or feel gratitude for. It does not have to be anything big. Something small will work as well, like the initial flicker that starts a fire. If you cannot find anything in your mind that can flip you to a positive emotion, then watching something funny or calling an uplifting friend may do the trick. The idea is to find something that will turn the wheel of your brain in a different direction. Finding something to smile about will help to break the negative loop while enlightening your perspective.

J. GOAL SETTING

The feeling of helplessness is a major reason people lack energy and motivation. Having a goal that seems entirely out of reach may become overwhelming on someone's mind. Splitting a big goal into a series of smaller ones is an excellent way to feel empowered and increase self-confidence. These smaller sub-goals should still feel challenging. You may not run a marathon today, but we can start by walking one mile. Your final goal may be to lose one hundred pounds, but if you don't yet believe you can lose that amount, you can begin by aiming to lose five pounds within a shorter period of time. Your mind will be able to believe you can achieve these smaller goals because they seem feasible. Once you trust you can do it, your brain will start generating energy and motivation. Also, it feels a lot better for your mind if you tell yourself that you will be eating healthy and exercising only for a shorter period of time instead of the longer term. This way, you keep moving forward one interval at a time.

These chunks of smaller accomplishments will give you the necessary self-confidence to pursue higher challenging goals in the following rounds. The more sub-goals you accomplish, the stronger the habits you are forming in your mind and spirit. This will also give you a stronger desire to accomplish bigger goals. The more you believe you can achieve it, the brighter outlook you will generate. In contrast, while in doubt about achieving your goal, your desire to obtain it creates an inner conflict that may originate feelings of defeat, reflected in very little energy and motivation.

II. BUILD THE HABIT OF TAKING ACTION

Action is one of the most significant sources that generate inner energy and motivation. If we need to lose 20 or 200 pounds, the strength of our desire will determine the efficacy of the method we use to lose weight. The person who wants to lose 20 pounds should not sit down and watch TV all day while eating fast food, just because the goal is 20 pounds. Instead, they need to imbibe the same self-discipline as the person who needs to lose 200 pounds. The bottom line is we need to commit to a strict and consistent healthy diet regimen and exercise routine; this will build a solid habit.

The plan of action to take depends on the type of target you are trying to achieve. The longer you do something, the higher the probability of creating a habit. Therefore, using the analogy above, if you do some exercise and eat healthy on and off, your 20 extra pounds will be with you for the long haul, lest you take the goal seriously

All goals can be split into two categories. The first category includes goals that are explicitly feasible to attain at this moment. Wanting a job in a specific company, playing for a specific sports team, or opening a business and having the necessary measurable skills and knowledge that makes you a qualified person for the desired position are examples within this category. The second category includes all your desires and goals, which are not feasible at this precise moment. For instance, buying a house, but you don't currently have a job or any savings.

The plan of action required for each of these categories will be different. Working on your self-confidence may do the trick if your goal belongs to the first category. For example, interviewing for a position within a company or sports team, where you will compete with many equally or even more qualified individuals, may require you to work on your self-confidence. What will determine who gets the position or gets the most clients is most likely the individual who believes in themselves, wants it the most, and has more self-confidence. A quick pick-me-up trick for an immediate self-confidence boost is to speak in a slightly higher tone than what you feel at that moment. You may want to check your body mode—standing straight and keeping your head up as if it were being held up by a string, keeping your ears, shoulders, and hips aligned while opening your chest. These are feasible short-term goals that are attainable at the moment. Give it a try. You can feel the positive energy that this body awareness and awakening can trigger.

If your goal belongs to the second category and is not immediately feasible, you need to understand everything about the requirements necessary to achieve that goal. For example, if you want to obtain financial wealth but don't have a job or business, it is doubtful that these economic benefits will appear immediately. However, you will need to start by building the skill or set of skills for a job or business that will enable you with a key to open the door for that financial path. In later chapters, we will discuss other strategies that combine tangibles and intangibles practices to maximize your chances of getting what you want sooner.

III. INCORPORATE A PERSONAL GROWTH SYSTEM INTO YOUR DAILY ROUTINE

There are many elements you can use for your personal growth. Listening to motivational speeches, reading, or listening to self-help books are quick ways to spark motivation and confidence, especially when you are in a stage where you cannot generate it yourself.

Another important element for self-growth that will

increase your motivation is spending time with individuals with a positive mindset. Suppose you have one of those days where everything seems gray, and you spend all your time with others who see everything gray or black. Your mind will accept this mood as ordinary reality. Instead, you should spend your time with constructive minds to break the gloomy cycle and start seeing everything brighter.

A good differentiator for an advantageous growth system is to practice silence, especially mind silence. Mind silence opens many doors within your consciousness and will shift your perceptions, passions, and sense of purpose.

IV. USING WHAT'S AVAILABLE NOW

Sometimes it is normal to feel you don't have everything you need to put your perfect plan into effect; no one does. Every successful and happy person takes risks. They make decisions based on their ability to perceive opportunities on anything around them. Your strength is believing that you can start your plan of action today with whatever you have. Even if you don't have anything tangible, you can start working on yourself by learning what's necessary for the direction you want to head towards. You can also start thinking about your different options and brainstorming possibilities, including reaching out to anybody who may be willing and able to help. The critical piece here is to take the first step forward so the energy can start flowing through your veins.

Once we plant an idea in our mind, our subconscious

will take over, and as long as we take action, it will drive us toward our target. Keeping our attitude focused on what we have and what we can do to move forward while not focusing on what we don't have is the secret to engineering solutions. Don't wait for the perfect time because perfection is relative to your state of mind. Keep reading, learning, and moving forward to your target. Sometimes, you will need to adjust or change your plan entirely, which is OK as you grow. And as long as you can keep your motivation ignited, you will find a solution for every challenge you face during your journey.

V. SETBACKS ARE PART OF THE JOURNEY

Be ready for lousy days and setbacks; everyone has them. A terrible day allows us to grow and become even better. The more setbacks and challenges we have and face with actions, the better we become at resolving them. A fall just means we are moving. No one who stays still ever falls, so knowing we will fail sometimes is a good thing. Every fall, our spirit, and character emerge stronger and ready for the next more ambitious challenge. The point is, we will face situations we never planned for, and in many cases, they will make us feel uncomfortable, drained, and discouraged. Pretending that unwanted events are not natural will be ludicrous, but facing them with determination shows personal growth and wisdom.

As life keeps moving and evolving, realities will keep changing and surprise us at times. Fortunately, we all have the power to choose how to handle any situation. We always have complete control over how we react to anything. Only we can decide what is available and how we'll use it to make the best of our current circumstances. Being open to adjustments allows us to make the best of what comes our way. Once we see these setbacks or bad days as a normal part of any path we take, we will be mentally ready when it shows up and quickly move on to finding a solution for it

VI. IDENTIFY YOUR PASSION

One of the secrets to building an unlimited source of motivation and positivism is passion. We can be passionate about more than one thing. Once we discover at least one of our passions and decide to work towards it, we can forget about a lack of energy. Once we discover we have a passion for something, we will have a self-replenishing fuel of determination and conviction that we are on the right path, with ease of mind.

Having a passion doesn't mean jumping back and forth every second of the day. Sure, it will give us a sense of self-purpose, motivation, creativity, and imagination to generate positive and joyful emotions. This will empower us to continue growing and building our character while enjoying most of the journey. Exercising one or more of our passions can be a love-hate relationship. I love my job as a Software Engineer so much that sometimes I dream about it. Many times, I cannot wait to get up so I can try out something new related to a piece of software or data that has been flowing in my mind. Time flies when I'm designing, building architecture, or developing something new.

When ideas emerge in my mind, they awaken and maintain a high level of energy.

Conversely, as part of the process, there are frustrations also; either because I didn't come up with the perfect idea or because the available technologies limit my concept. As a result, my excitement towards the task diminishes. All these emotions are part of my passion cycle.

The secret is to find other ways to do something when the first approach does not work. I know that with every new cycle, excitement and frustration will be part of the adventure. It is normal to get stuck from time to time while achieving anything. We just need to keep trying a different approach until we find the right solution when that happens. Once we figure it out, the excitement will fill our minds and soul again. This is a continuous loop driven by passion, and it is the same or very similar for everyone who finds their passion. These feelings can not be bought. This is what makes it so special. It is one of those things that no one can live for you.

Being passionate doesn't stop challenges from coming your way. But it makes it easier to find the motivation to overcome them. You, like me, have a passion for something, even if you haven't discovered what that "something" is yet. To identify your passion, it helps by asking yourself, "What activity do I perform and lose track of time while doing it?" "What things bring me excitement and motivation?" "What activity or thoughts provide me with a sense of purpose?" When asking yourself these questions, you must be honest with yourself. If you loved to play baseball when you were growing up, you likely see yourself full of excitement with the thought of being a professional baseball player. But, if you are outside of the normal age range to become a professional baseball player, it would be best to concentrate on achieving objectives and dreams that are more feasible to your current state—perhaps considering engaging in other activities or businesses that have some relation to what you love.

Knowing what you like and dislike and trying out new things will help you isolate your options. Don't feel discouraged if you find you don't enjoy doing anything you think of at the moment. The more you identify areas you dislike, the closer you get to identifying the things you enjoy most. Once you find it, it will expand and invigorate all areas of your lives. Passion gives you the required energy to go the extra mile without complaining but rather enjoying the ride. Being passionate about your goals will make your mind open to gaining new knowledge. It will enable you to live your present to the fullest. Your life will become a constant appreciation of what you have and the people around you. Your concept of happiness and success will change from a destination to a journey.

Once you know those inner drivers and tendencies, the next step is to get deeper into the specifics. There is a lot of data available about industries, jobs, and a career in line with those tendencies. Furthermore, I believe going to places where you can see first-hand people performing those activities is of great value in expanding your horizons. Suppose you have an altruistic tendency to serve others or perhaps feel the need to make a difference within politics; going to the places where you can see individuals doing what you think you love would be a great learning opportunity. Another example of an inclination of your passion could be loving to be surrounded by people versus being alone. This may be a sign that you enjoy things that have larger groups of people involved. Whether you find pleasure in figuring things out or being creative with your hand, being your boss, working within a strict environment with a clear list of defined tasks and schedules, or enjoying a flexible environment with more time and access to creativity, finding your passion is rewarding. It can be more challenging for some than others, but it is a life change and all worth it in the end.

How Words Impact Your Game

When we interact, part of the first impression we make and perceive comes from the way we speak. Words, and more importantly, the intonation of those words, will have a positive or negative impact on every relationship we establish.

All generations have used words to communicate feelings and emotions. The national anthems, poems, motivational speeches, beautiful songs, and even malicious and harmful words impact people's lives. Within each generation, some individuals have used words to trigger positive changes in the world, while others have used them to manipulate, hurt, and create other destructive conditions. We have all said something that we wish we could take back. But unfortunately, once words leave our mouths, there is no way to bring them back. More importantly, if these words were said to someone publicly or privately, or in the media, they could haunt us for a long time.

The OΣU will guide you to use words in constructive

ways to avoid getting into situations that bring you regrets. Our words are like a business card to people who don't know us. At the same time, words with no actions and words expressing the opposite of what we feel won't have the same impactful meaning. We cannot reverse anything we have said, so it is essential to watch what we say from this point forward. Your words matter; they represent who you are.

While playing your game, you will be using two different strategies to manage the impact of words. These strategies are Outgoing words and Incoming words. During the outgoing words process, you are in total control of what you say. Each of us has a repertory of words that we commonly use as part of our vocabulary. This outcome represents which part of us is winning the OΣU. Each constructive word coming out of someone portrays that the productive force in them is winning. On the contrary, when someone speaks words of hate and hurtful statements, their destructive power wins.

The incoming words strategy is a whole new game. We have no control over what anyone says to us. But we have full power to choose how to react to them. We already know that we cannot force someone else to be the way we want, just like we cannot control what someone says. Recognizing and accepting this will save us many unnecessary arguments and frustrations when dealing with family, friends, and other relationships. The significance of incoming words is proportional to the value we give to them. The other person only has as much power as we give them to affect our emotions, thoughts, and actions.

If we have a friend that makes us feel bad every time

they're around, we need to understand why they have such power over us. And if we cannot avoid this feeling after each interaction with such a person, then minimizing those interactions can be the correct solution. Our subconscious mind keeps gathering information and saving knowledge related to what we are thinking and saying. The words we say to ourselves and others during conversations, arguments, or gossip will generate emotions that eventually trigger particular actions.

Thoughts can be challenging to control. Nevertheless, we have complete control over the words we choose to say, independent of what we think. This doesn't make us a hypocrite; it is meant to maintain a constructive posture, especially during the times we are experiencing negative thoughts and emotions. We will have a much better way to convey our words once our feelings are stable.

All heated arguments can be prevented if at least one of the parties involved stops talking and listens to what the other is saying. It is essential to understand the reason and the expected outcome when engaging in a debate. If it is not clear to us, it's better to drop it before finding ourselves with regretful consequences. Recognizing that other people's words only have the value, we decide to give them will save us from unnecessary negative emotions.

Many people spend hours each day gossiping about others and complaining about everything that happens to them when they could use their time to create a plan of action towards the change they are looking for. When someone comes to us with gossip or other unconstructive conversation, we can quiet our minds and avoid engagement. Welcoming a gossipy or detrimental dialogue will open the door for more of the same, creating a cycle of negative emotions. Negative criticism, unhelpful comments, and behaviors that don't bring up anything positive for us or anyone else can ruin all types of relationships.

Many people have a deep-rooted habit of complaining. They complain about their jobs, spouses, kids, elected officials; they complain just about everything. There is only one single rule in getting rid of a complaint: Do something about it. That is it. There is no magic formula. If we don't like something, then we need to do something constructive about it. Let us not confuse being a complainer with using our voice for things that matter. There are situations in which our voice is all we have to trigger change.

Your words are the representation of who you are and who you want to be. Choosing your words carefully and making sure they communicate the message that represents who you are will make a significant difference in how you feel about yourself.

How Playing the OΣU Can Change Your Life

When I started working in the technical industry, I noticed that many professionals tended to change jobs within the first few years, so I decided to research this phenomenon for my master's degree thesis. My topic for the research was on IT (Information Technology) turnover. I wanted to know what made employees leave or stay in their current jobs. I was very interested in learning what incentives could make a difference for individuals to stay or leave their jobs and measure their current level of satisfaction.

My studies revealed that the highest level of satisfaction occurred between the ages of 25-34. Unless an individual occupies a higher power position, there was a decline in satisfaction as the years passed. In terms of incentives, money was the highest incentive to make people within this same age group change jobs. Base pay, challenging environments, and opportunities to grow were the top three motivators and differentiators for a person to stay or change their current job, independent of their age group. These factors were followed by the desire for recognition and other non-financial incentives. The high-level summary of my research showed that most employees were unhappy with their current state of affairs. One interesting factor I noticed was that for many, despite changing their jobs, they would quickly reach a level of dissatisfaction again. What does this tell us? It's like the saying, "the grass isn't greener on the other side." Money and other financial incentives are great, but they will only take us so far. It does not matter how many times we move from our grass to the next greener one. If we don't learn how to water and nourish it, we will keep finding ourselves with the same level of dissatisfaction. The best way to nurture our grass is to be fully aware of our passion and choices. Once our decisions are in line with pursuing a defined goal, we will become keen about our decision-making, which will make our quest much more satisfying.

It doesn't matter where you are, what you have, or who you are, as long as you are happy, satisfied, and grateful for who you have become. If you are not, then accept the challenge of playing this game, and in 63-days, your life will turn its helm for a promising transformation of building the foundation to become the most satisfied and happy version you can be.

THE 9 GUIDELINES

All games have rules, and the 0ΣU is no exception. These rules and guidelines will help keep you on track for success. We are all playing a role in a 0ΣU, whether ours or someone else's. Those who don't know the rules become easy targets for others to take advantage of. There is nothing wrong with being part of another person's game, as long as you are aware and make the decisions that are best for you.

GUIDELINE ONE
EMBRACING THE THREE A'S

One principle oversees all others: Embrace the Three A's: Awareness, Action, and Accountability.

If you decide to play this game and want to ensure success, you must pay special attention to this rule. You can follow all others, which will help you achieve tangible objectives, but without owning the three A's, you won't get to the level of living a life without regrets and a life with a sense of fulfillment and gratitude.

I. AWARENESS

This principle implies that you are required to be in an active state of consciousness. Maintaining your awareness will help you identify when thoughts and emotions may be driving you to the wrong course of action, even before their execution.

This game does not care about judging your actions as right or wrong because it intends to enable you to build your personalized strategy based on your unique potential. Still, the game expects that you maintain the rule of awareness because it is the main guideline that can prevent you from engaging in activities that you regret.

First, as we know, no one is perfect. People are not robots, so it is natural for mistakes to occur at any time. Your awareness plays a significant role in the number of errors you make, their severity, and your ability to recover from them. Living under the state of awareness is like exercising the muscle that builds ownership. The more you activate your awareness, the more you will feel ownership of all your outcomes. Awareness removes the veil through which you perceive your life. Without this veil, it is doubtful that you will see yourself as a victim of circumstance.

Living without regrets does not mean living entirely according to social norms, but rather, living in a way where you do not compromise your actions with your core values. It means taking control of your actions so you don't blame others when things don't go your way. There are many examples of people behaving without awareness of their actions. Often, these behaviors have tremendous consequences, such as the loss of relationships, jobs, self-respect, and dignity. Sometimes these results are so embarrassing that they feel powerless to overcome them, and unfortunately, some of them end their own lives as a result. We can find such examples on social networks, in videos related to drugs, sexual activities, and other times when individuals take huge insane risks due to peer pressure. In all of these cases, there is a common denominator. The individuals behave in a way, relinquishing their control, and compromising their core values.

Some people learn their lessons after facing the consequences of engaging in such activities. While others don't learn anything as they have become accustomed to getting themselves involved in such behaviors. Although the tangible and visual results would be the same in both scenarios, the mental and emotional results between the two individuals are quite different. Keeping your awareness before engaging in any activity may make the difference between living with fulfillment and pride and becoming a pawn in someone else's game.

II. ACTIONS

Actions are the second principle of the three A's. When we see the word action at once, we imagine physical activities. Study, work, walk, run, everything we physically engage in can be seen and measured in one way or another.

The OΣU uses the principle of "Actions" to oversee both tangible physical activities and intangible activities, like the art of thinking. The act of thought management is critical in changing habits and shaping your emotions to make them work for you. The better you get at managing your thoughts, the better you will see your quality of life. Thoughts are intangible actions that go hand in hand with physical actions. Nothing will ever be invented or built without good ideas, and nothing will ever be created or constructed without tangible actions. One cannot succeed without the other. This principle ensures that you are mentally ready before committing to any course of physical action. Learning to manage how you think is the difference between acting and reacting to a particular event and a successful outcome.

All actions, tangible and intangible, need to be strengthened, focused, balanced, and aligned for success. How often do people go to the gym or practice different activities to strengthen their bodies while neglecting the mind? When playing the zero-sum game [of you], you will learn useful techniques to enhance your mind as well as your body.

Thanks to the people who have learned to balance their mental activities with their physical actions, everything we see around us was created. The future is being made, RIGHT NOW. Your future is in your hands, RIGHT NOW! The future of our cities, countries, and society is in the making from our collective thoughts and actions.

III. ACCOUNTABILITY

Accountability is the final principle of the three A's. This rule brings everything together. I love this principle, and I hope you will too. Perhaps not initially, because it will set off a sentiment of self-defense in the initial phase. But once you get over this hurdle, it will completely change how you perceive and live your life. This principle says, "we are the only one responsible for our outcomes." Consequences come from your decisions and from your lack of decisions, the results of your actions and inactions. Furthermore, it includes the way you use your power to impart fortune to others.

Perhaps you are starting your game with zero currency, or you are financially wealthy. Maybe you are beginning with a lot of emotional support or none. You might have an excellent education or business right now or nothing other than your inner desire for change. You may be unaware that you want something more or something that will give you a more profound sense of fulfillment. Regardless of where you are and what you have, realizing that these outcomes are because of your decisions, or lack thereof, mold your present. As you move forward in your zero-sum game, your decisions will now mold your future according to what you really want.

A few years ago, I came across an article about parenting that caught my attention. I read the paragraph explaining why kids tend to blame their mother, father, or guardian for every situation that gives them emotional pain, embarrassment, or discomfort. The author explained that the child expects the parent to shield them from any problems that could cause them distress. This is an expectation that happens automatically within the child's mind. After reading this article, it made me realize how this behavior can stay with someone after those childhood days.

As we get older, using excuses and blaming others provide the same sense of shielding we felt when we were kids. I remember my excuses when I got a lousy grade, especially during my middle school years. The reason was always an external event or someone else other than me. Some individuals never grow out of these childhood behaviors. By their adulthood, they have mastered the blame game. Thus they find excuses for everything. Once a person gets comfortable using excuses, it will become a natural part of their behavior.

People with this mindset will complain about work, clients, bosses, management, co-workers, benefits, business culture, politics, etc. They will find issues with family, spouses, kids, and friends in their social circles. They will also complain about their bad luck and all the injustice they have been subjected to. Unfortunately, they perceive all their obstacles as the results of external circumstances and actions from other people. This is a precise recipe for distancing further away from the actual source of their problem; themselves.

Over the years, I have witnessed how one fact can be seen through two different lenses, creating two contrasting realities. A popular justification is "opportunities," to be more precise, the "lack of opportunities." I have seen individuals born in the United States complaining because, according to them, better benefits are given to people from other countries. On the same subject, I have seen individuals who have come to the USA from other countries complaining about the lack of opportunities because they were not born in the US. It is easy to see that both realities are the product of each individual's perception. There are opportunities and challenges for everyone. Still, it is always easier to find excuses outside and blame others when we cannot change ourselves and take ownership of our outcomes.

Taking ownership and accountability for your present situation and recognizing that you can learn from past erroneous actions can be challenging. The main reason is that your ego usually gets involved, and in many cases, it makes you refuse to recognize you were at fault. If you start experiencing this type of emotion, that is a good thing. Let the feeling engulf you. The feeling of self-defense gives you the opportunity for self-growth. Overcoming this feeling will give you a sense of freedom and self-respect, giving you a different view when making future decisions.

The OΣU will coach you to reach your targets by using your thoughts and emotions to trigger the proper actions. Thoughts by themselves will take you nowhere. Uncontrollable emotions can make you subjective and unstable. Acts without guidance and motive won't give you self-satisfaction. Once you learn to manage the T.E.A. cycle (thoughts, emotions, and actions), you will find opportunities in places you didn't notice before.

By the time you have completed and won the OΣU game, you will recognize that you are the primary cause of the outcome you get. There will be no more feelings of victimization, and you will see that there is no one responsible for your well-being or misfortune other than yourself. You must take full accountability for your life. You are where you are because of you. And, you have what you have because you allowed it. Of course, there are some exceptions to this, like sexual assault, abuse, hate crimes, racism, and other cases where someone has taken complete advantage of you; where you didn't have many options to respond or get out of that situation on your own.

Some of us have lived through horrible experiences. And I wish we could go back in time and fix those cases to eliminate the deep suffering our souls had to endure. Unfortunately, none of us has that power, so the only constructive alternative is to move on. There is no gain in dwelling on the past, independent of how we got where we are now. Whatever happened is already done, and we must forge ahead. The future is yet to come, and today is all we have to start building a better future.

Like with everything else, you have more than one choice. You can put this book down and continue down a path you are familiar with or accept the challenge to play this game while taking ownership of everything about yourself. You can make an incredible difference for the rest of your life.

GUIDELINE TWO
ASSESSMENT OF OUR "AS-IS" STATE

In business and project management, there is a concept of "As-Is" and "To-Be" to refer to a project's current condition or process and its desired future vision. Before re-engineering them, it is essential to understand all the features, capabilities, and weaknesses of the existing project, process, software, or feature we are trying to change.

The importance of understanding the current process is mainly for two reasons. The first one is to make sure we preserve all the features that are working as desired. The second reason is to avoid reinventing the wheel. Nobody likes to waste a lot of time, effort, and money rebuilding something only to realize that the new construct has no added value to the pre-existing way of doing business.

We can implement the same "As-Is"/" To-Be" concept into our personal life choices. This process will give us an objective perspective of where we are today and where we want to be.

Before we start playing OΣU, let's create an inventory of our current resources. The things we wish to have and the things others have are irrelevant for this analysis. Our "As-Is" state covers all characteristics of WHAT we have and WHO we are at this point. Our health, financial status, educational status, character, emotional state, habits, skills, tangible resources, knowledge, and beliefs are part of this assessment.

Let's start by writing down our list of current resources. For some of us, the first answer will be, "I don't have anything. I don't have money, support, or any other resource to help me." We might have other variations of this feeling of hopelessness. This could be because we think we have tried everything and that nothing works or may feel overwhelmed due to the number of obstacles out of our control.

The reality is, you, me, and everyone else have to face different difficulties as part of living. Our obstacles are just challenges along the way that shows we are making progress. If we keep a positive and constructive attitude, we will see them as an opportunity for growth. Unless we live in a bubble that stays still, it is natural to face drawbacks as we move forward. All these hurdles will test our strength and growth so we can achieve greater success.

Let's not confuse overcoming challenges with accepting a life of constant struggle due to lack of action. Inaction is not an obstacle; it is a decision, and we are the only ones that can do something about it. Getting stuck and feeling victimized, angry, hopeless, or ungrateful are choices we make. We can spend hours, days, and our entire life justifying our lack of decision-making. This attitude might buy a person an elapse of empathy from friends and family, but none of that will help anyone to be happy and confident.

In the initial phase of OΣU, we will answer a list of questions to help us recognize the available resources right now, which can assist in the journey. This includes how we interact with other people, our way of thinking, and the type of actions we take. It will also baseline the amount of expertise we've gained over the years and all the specifics concerning our goals. It further comprises defining our inner circle or support group, which may or may not include our immediate family and our closest friends. Furthermore, our hobbies and any other activity we do in our spare time must be identified and documented as well.

Before proceeding, I want you to take a pen and paper or any electronic device and jot down the things which will assist in describing the current state of affairs. The purpose is to find answers to the "What?" and the "Why?" of your objectives. Once you know the reason behind what you want and why you want it, you will move to the next step and answer the "How?" The "how" will help you come up with a plan of action to achieve your target.

Begin this process by thinking of something you have tried to achieve without success up to this point. Now, answer these questions:

- What is your goal?
- Why do you want to achieve this goal?
- How are you trying to obtain it?

Make a list of all the activities you have engaged in towards achieving this target. This list should include all actions, mental and physical.

Now, look at your existing plan of action.

- What do you think has prevented you from attaining this objective?
- How many hours per day do you dedicate to achieving this specific goal, and what specific tasks do you do during that time?
- Do you believe you have the necessary skills to succeed?
- If your objective is related to a business, do you know what the competition is doing? Do you see what others

have done to succeed, and what has made others fail?
- Name the people you spend most of your free time with.
- How many books or documentaries have you read or listened to within the past month? What percentage of these books, documentaries, or any other reliable information relates to one of the various aspects of your intended target?
- State how much time you spend acquiring skills and building strategies related to your goal vs. the time you spend engaging in other activities that add no value to your objectives

Please write down as much as you can. Once you are done, keep these notes close by, you will be referring to them once you begin designing your "To-Be" state.

GUIDELINE THREE
IDENTIFY OUR CORE PRIORITIES

After identifying your current state of affairs and before setting up your goals for your zero-sum game, it is critical to understand your priorities. When setting priorities, people often rush the process; they set up goals without taking the time to determine what keeps their lives in balance. Setting up priorities is as important as setting up goals. If you ask a large group of people what they want to set up as their first goal, many responses will be about financial freedom. But then, if you ask a follow -up question about what they are willing to give up for that, silence is usually the response.

Understanding your core priorities is vital, so if you don't undertake the time to identify your core priorities, you will cross the line and compromise your core values. The most common priorities are faith, family, finances, recognition, friends, social causes, fame, work, and free time. Their order varies for each individual. If your core priority is family, you should not take a job that requires you to work 20-hours a day, even if the salary is very enticing. However, if your number one priority is financial freedom, no matter the "cost," you may be willing to take a job that offers substantial financial incentives. Nonetheless, you should be ready to deal with sacrificing other areas of your life for your core priorities. For example, chasing financial freedom could result in your family and other personal areas suffering from your absence or lack of time.

The next thing you need to do is set up the priority ranking for each. Understanding where you are and where you want to be in 1, 2,5, and 10 years can help define your priority list and ranking.

During my teen years, I started searching for topics related to the meaning of life. I wanted to know the primary questions which I think every human has sought at some point or another. I wanted to know if there was a God and the main purpose of life. These questions got me into researching different books on science and religion. I bought a multitude of books and went to libraries to read and study other theories on psychology, metaphysics, meditation, and energies in general. My research led me in various directions—each one offering me a different perspective. Even though many concepts were very intriguing, the fact is, I did not find one concrete answer to my questions, at least not in an objective way.

The thirst for that kind of knowledge was intense for about six years. As I learned more theories and understood various complexities among different cultures, some of my original beliefs and cultural roots changed. One of the positive things that came about from my quest is that I got a better sense of myself and understood the things that had more worth from my perspective. At the time, I thought I had discovered the puzzle of life, but little did I know it was only the beginning of my learning experience.

A good old friend of mine was very persistent and determined to attain financial freedom. He mastered the skill of positive thinking and surrounded himself with a very positive support group. He began to flourish. But his success got to his ego. He proved to himself and others how easy it was to make money by controlling his thinking and through a set of determining actions. As more money flowed, he began to feel invincible. He lost his humility. Now, as his financial status kept rising, his family began falling apart at a rapid rate. A couple of years later, he ended up worse than he was financially than before he started his journey. He lost his family and most of his friends. If he had set the right priorities from the beginning, most likely, he would have ended up very well financially and with a happy family.

I firmly believe that pursuing a single target for which you have passion and hunger is always attainable, but you must be aware of the price to pay for it. Having a clear understanding of the activities involved in your pursuit can level your expectations. It is unfortunate if you commit to being miserable for a long time with the idea that you will be happy once you reach your target. If you never make it to that end, you will regret living your life doing something you disliked or, worse yet, hated because you only had your mind focused on the end result and not the journey; and what you were willing to give up along the journey.

Shortly after coming to the United States of America, there was a time when financial stability was my highest priority. I remember researching different jobs based solely on financial incentives. This is how I got into the technical field. It just so happened that once I got in the field, I fell in love with it. As I got older and had my children, money became less relevant, and my immediate family became my number one priority. It was crystal clear to me that I would never let anything or anyone take precedence over this priority. Understanding the value of everything that mattered most to me helped me make better decisions regarding my career and social life. I have to say. I faced difficult choices when I had to bypass great financial opportunities to retain my number one priority. I passed up fantastic economic incentives greater than four times my income at the time. Nevertheless, up to this point, each one of these decisions has been worth it because my family remained my top priority.

Your priorities can be completely different from mine, and that is perfectly OK. What is important is that you take the time to define the list and order of everything that matters to you. Being clear about them will prevent you from making the wrong decisions that otherwise could bring you deep regrets later. Setting up priorities and defining goals that bring you balance is key to feeling gratitude and experiencing life to the fullest.

GUIDELINE FOUR
DESIGN AND ARCHITECT THE "TO-BE" STATE

Have you ever started driving a car without having a destination? My guess is no. Unless someone is confused or wants to spend time alone, there is no logical reason to start driving without a final point. You may not know all the details of how to get there, you may need to use a map, you may even need to ask strangers along the way, but before you start your car's engine, you already know your destination.

Have you heard of anyone that got lost forever while trying to find an address? Of course, the answer is no. It might take a long time and a lot of struggle, it may also be possible the driver might have gone in circles a few times, perhaps the car broke down, or they got a flat tire, or maybe the driver got pulled over by the police for speeding and got a ticket. These obstacles and many others could slow the driver from getting to the destination, but eventually, they will get there. It is as simple as that. Once you know your goal, nothing can stop you or block your path, FOREVER.

As the sole Architect and Engineer of your life, take this time to lay out what you want; this is your "To-Be" state. Notice that the concept here is to design and not only to define. Defining is better known by the idea of describing something, which is a passive activity. Designing something enables you to be creative and perceive more critical details in your imagination. All this contributes to coming up with a more specific plan of action. When designing your goal, you will generate ideas in your mind and combine them with a plan of action. For the OΣU, creating your To-Be state of affairs will cover five sections: Self-growth, Obtaining knowledge, Relationships, Job, and Time Management. You may add other areas that are specific to your desired lifestyle.

It is vital to allow the leading force within you to design your To-Be state. Doing so will allow you to contain everything you desire without limiting beliefs (from the ideal relationship to the optimum source of income). Be aware that during this exercise, the opposing side in you may want to take control. It will try to sabotage your goal setting by planting self-doubt. You must ignore it and ensure that your positive side is the only one active at this moment. Let your mind wander as if you were in a dream. When you are dreaming, your mind accepts any possibility without resistance. To architect your To-Be state or desired future, you must see your desires as reachable and believable in your mind.

I. DESIGNING YOUR "TO-BE" STATE FOR SELF GROWTH

The way we care about ourselves has a real impact on all areas of our lives and those around us. Often, we don't take the time to make sure our minds and bodies are performing at their best. As lack of time increases and we get more responsibilities and demands from our current lifestyle, we pay the price by ignoring the needs of our body and mind. More importantly, the quality of our relationships, job and business performance, and sense of fulfillment are all negatively affected when we neglect ourselves.

A. THE 80/20 RULE

The Pareto Principle states that most of the results we get (80%) come from a 20% cause. Vilfredo Pareto was a late nineteenth century economist/sociologist who first noted and reported that about 80 percent of wealth was concentrated in about 20 percent of a population. This principle is the basis for what we now call the Pareto Principle (Sanders, 1987).

In the 0ΣU, you will be implementing the Pareto Principle concept to become more productive while putting in less effort. Notice that the point here is to be more effective and happier, and more accomplished during the process. Anyone can achieve anything that becomes the focus of the mind and soul. However, doing so while living your present state of being and enjoying the path to your To-be state is different. Using the 80/20 rule as part of this game means dedicating around 20% of the twenty-four hours you have in a day to strengthen your foundation. This means taking care of yourself and bringing balance to your day-to-day activities. Taking care of your mind and body will ensure that you have the best possible health while ensuring your mind feels stable and balanced.

The Pareto Principle is not an exact law, sometimes it could be 70/30 or 90/10, but in most cases, 80/20 is a good average to target. Twenty-four hours are available to everyone every day. You may need between 5-9 hours of sleep to feel rested. That leaves the remainder of the day for you to create your balance. So, how can you put the 80/20 rule to your advantage? 20% is about 3.5 of your awake hours. This means you should take part of this time for internal growth and maintaining a healthy body. It's best to find a physical activity that can be part of your daily routine. It does not need to be strenuous. Going for a walk, dancing, playing a sport, or doing anything that gets your heart pumping for at least 10-15 minutes can work wonders in your health. The objective here is not your physical appearance, even though that is a good bonus, but the clarity and energy you get in your mind during and after exercising. This will also help you to keep some diseases away. The remaining time of 20% should be dedicated to activities related to your top two priorities. We will discuss this further within the following chapters.

Below is an example of implementing the 20% of the 80/20 rule to create a healthy mind-body balance.

1. Start by waking up fifteen to thirty minutes before your average time.
2. Inhale and exhale three times slowly.

While still in bed, set up a few intentions for the day. For example, "I will see the good that exists in everything and everyone around me." "What can I do today to add more value to my (business, job, learning)?"

Another intention that will motivate you and baseline your day with full accountability is the following: "What activity can I do today to improve my relationship with my (spouse, child, parent, partner, friend, co-worker)?" "I am successful and thriving in everything I engage in."

This next intention will keep you focused on your objectives for the day while helping you manage your emotions and responses to unwanted adverse events. "I think, pause, act... when something unwanted happens." "While I am not in full control of circumstances blocking my way, I am always in control of choosing the way I deal with them."

3. Finish your intentions by planting a seed of gratitude, trusting that you will obtain your specific wishes or better. Repeat a few times, "Thank you. Thank you. Thank you."

4. Once you complete setting up your intentions, go out for a walk, or engage in any exercise for at least twenty minutes.

5. You can use your commuting time for self-development. I love audiobooks, and these days there are plenty of varieties to choose from. Listening to a positive and constructive book or podcast while traveling is perfect for decreasing stress, boosting self-confidence, and creating a harmonious mindset for the day.

6. During the day, it is essential to be kind in all activities you engage in and in all conversations you have while maintaining your own identity and position on what

you stand for.

7. At the end of the day and before going to sleep, it is beneficial to take five or ten minutes to pay attention to your feelings. Ask yourself, "How do I feel today?" "Are my feelings more positive than yesterday?" "Is there anything I want to make better tomorrow?"

Repeat this process for a week and review how the week goes. A week is usually enough to start experiencing improvements in the areas you care for.

I. THE BODY

Each one of us has only one body for the rest of our lives. Our physical body enables us to perform and experience all the activities we enjoy doing. It is a sophisticated resource that allows our mind and spirit to fulfill and maximize our enjoyment.

We often take our bodies for granted. We don't give it enough attention or care. We prevent it from performing at its highest potential by depriving it of a healthy diet and exercise. Despite all of this, our bodies keep operating to the best of their ability to help us march forward. If we starve our body trying to achieve an unhealthy form of skinny, our body will react by shutting down some processes in some areas to give enough supplement to the heart and brain as a last resort. When a person overeats saturated fats and refined sugar, it becomes challenging for the arteries in the body to get the blood to the proper places. Consuming drugs, smoking, and excessive alcohol is like poisoning the body and cells as they work so hard for us.

You alone can decide what you eat, drink, and do for pleasure. Remember that your body and mind are your best allies. Your mind and body depend on you to make the right decisions and provide them with what they need to perform at maximum capacity. You need your body to experience enjoyable and pleasurable activities.

Our culture, family, society, and peers have influenced how we see and think about our bodies. As important as it is to understand and support what our body needs, it is essential not to become obsessed over it for the wrong reasons. Some of the man-made rules within our cultures and society provide the fictional notion of a perfect body for a woman or a man. This misleading perception has contributed immensely to eating disorders for many teenagers and young adults and unnecessary cosmetic surgeries that further weaken their self-esteem. I am not suggesting that all cosmetic surgery is wrong. However, I believe that people should work on their self-esteem and confidence first, then decide whether having plastic surgery will make them happier. I want to emphasize that making these decisions should be based on the individual's specific motives, not because they are trying to fit into some misleading standards that make them lose their internal fortitude. Nurturing our inner strength and self-confidence will reflect the most beautiful and influential image you can ever have, and it will fill your soul with a sense of contentedness and fulfillment.

In terms of health, there is a lot of information out there about healthy diets and exercise routines. Doing crash diets is not sustainable, and it can leave the individual unmotivated in the process. Finding a balanced diet that works for you is best. Portion control is more sustainable than many other diet regimens. The reason is, your body and mind get used to the portions and send signals to be satisfied after consuming enough calories without going overboard. If you are used to eating abnormally large volumes of food, try to cut down the amount by a third and continue eating a little less every week until you feel satisfied when eating the proper amount. I like combining a balanced diet with some fasting because it helps my mental clarity, decreases my body inflammation, and increases my energy level.

If you look at yourself in the mirror and view your body as an asset or capital, you will see how you need to take care of that asset so you don't lose it. The body works very hard for us, and we need to show some gratitude in return by taking care of it to the best of our abilities.

2. THE MIND

We feed our minds through data, information, images, sounds, thoughts, ideas, learning skills, awareness, experience, and interactions. Our brain needs to be able to operate at its maximum capacity. I have found a few things to be very helpful in keeping the mind productive and motivated. The first thing is to filter the amount and type of information we expose our minds to regularly. Images, data, and interaction with others will also influence our thoughts and perceptions. Similarly to maintaining healthy food consumption for the body, we should be more selective of the information we feed our brains.

Another good strategy to keep your brain challenged is by learning new things. Every new skill and new knowledge you obtain helps to keep your brain in shape. Suppose you keep your mind interacting with constructive knowledge and ideas; you will feel triggers to perform significantly different actions than when you expose your mind to constant negative thoughts, destructive behaviors, and images. Choosing the information and expositions you give to your mind is like picking the seeds you want to grow in your garden. If you plant oranges, you will not get plantains; the same way, your mind will create more thoughts and emotions in reaction to the information and environment you expose it to.

In one of the science magazines I read, if we brush our teeth or brush our hair with the non-prevalent hand, we exercise different areas of our brain that would be otherwise inactive. After reading this, I began using my left hand (I am right-handed) to brush my teeth and write notes. This process was prolonged and frustrating. A few years after, I tore a muscle around my right elbow area, for which I had surgery to repair it. After the surgery, I had a cast on my right arm. Therefore, I couldn't use it for a few weeks. During my healing process, I was forced to use my left hand for daily tasks. This time I noticed, I became incredibly efficient with my left hand. This time was different despite all the struggles and unsuccessful trials when previously practicing as a mental exercise. It was as if my brain took over and gave the proper orders to the left arm to perform its new duties. I admit this was amazing to me, primarily because of two reasons: first, I was never this efficient when I previously tried, and second, this time, it seemed to have happened overnight. Writing with my left hand got a lot faster and the writing more legible. I brushed my teeth and hair with no problem, and my posture improved because I stopped leaning in the wrong direction. To me, this was proof of the beautiful gift we all possess: our brain/mind.

II. DESIGNING YOUR "TO-BE" STATE FOR RELATIONSHIPS

The people we spend most of our time with will influence our lives one way or another. Generally, we are attracted to people with similar values; otherwise, creating and maintaining communication is challenging. In most cases, one person may be attracted to another only because it feels good. This feeling of joy, when it is sincere, generates positive emotions on both sides.

Having a support group will encourage us when we feel helpless or tired. This group is not a place to find sympathy and compliance for our excuses but instead a place with candid and constructive criticism and support. We all go through painful or frustrating moments, which makes our self-energy source drop. As a result, we may not see things clearly. Our support group must be made up of reliable people. There should be transparency; that is, everyone should come as they are, no pretense. It is a safe group; everyone knows the other person's strengths and weaknesses, but there is a common goal of positivism and constructive comfort.

Feeling similarities in innate vibrations is very different from showing interest in another person for calculated reasons. If you decide to play the 0ΣU, you should be aware that manipulating others to your advantage will affect the cause-effect course of our outcomes. The reason is simple; the thought, emotion, and action cycle are in constant motion, and they generate patterns that affect your character and the person you are becoming. Keep in mind that the goal isn't just to get what you want, but rather to get it while feeling grateful and fulfilled. These components are vital to living a life of joy, consciousness, and gratitude while minimizing regrets.

A. BUILD A SUPPORT GROUP

There is a direct correlation between the people we spend or interact with most of our free time and how we conduct and think about ourselves. Building a support group means identifying with the people and other sources to influence our ideas and decision-making.

Jim Rohn has a famous quote, "We are the average of the five people we spend the most time with." While I don't entirely agree with him, I believe that everyone is very similar to the closest people they spend their free time with. An individual who spends much of their time with a bully or arrogant and shallow person will have a very different set of values than a person who believes in fairness and justice. If you spend much of your time with people that complain about anything and everything, it will be tough for you to maintain a positive point of view about your circumstances.

I found an interesting study about how obesity has increased in past decades. This study took place for about thirty years, starting in 1971. This group of doctors wanted to scientifically determine the correlation between obesity and the possible factors that spread to multiple degrees of separation from the obese individual. The study evaluated over twelve thousand people, multiple times over the thirty years, using longitudinal statistical models to examine the weight gain in a person and the association to their friends, family, and neighbors. The study showed that a person's chance of becoming obese increased by 57% when a friend became obese. In the case of siblings, the probability of one sibling becoming obese increased by 40% if another became obese. This study also demonstrated neighborhood influence, especially the co-relations between the same sexes within close vicinity.

The study concluded that "Network phenomena appear to be relevant to the biologic and behavioral trait of obesity, and obesity appears to spread through social ties. These findings have implications for clinical and public health interventions." Source: https://www.nejm.org/doi/full/10.1056/NEJMsa066082

In a similar study, these doctors researched the extent of the person-to-person spread of smoking behavior and the extent to which smokers would influence others to smoke. This study also concluded that "Network phenomena appear to be relevant to smoking cessation. Smoking behavior spreads through close and distant social ties, groups of interconnected people stop smoking in concert, and smokers are increasingly marginalized

SOURCE

1. https://www.nejm.org/doi/full/10.1056/NEJMsa066082

socially." Source https://www.nejm.org/doi/full/10.1056/ NEJMsa0706154

We can find the effect of association everywhere. One of my loved ones had a problem with alcohol; it started with social drinking in his late teens and early twenties, then continued and became a destructive habit as years passed. He attempted to stop drinking several times. However, his friends were all drinkers at the time, so each time he tried to quit, he would only end up drinking again. Eventually, we lost him due to complications in his liver.

We may not be able to choose every person who works with us or select each individual in our classroom or any social event we participate in, but we have the full power to choose who we spend our time with. I'm not suggesting staying away from others due to physical attributes. However, I want to create awareness about how the influence process works. If you are aware of it, you will be better prepared to protect yourself from damaging influences and may be able to help others break the cycle.

Understanding the power of association enables you to build a constructive support group to motivate and feel motivated. One of my beautiful soul friends, Simonetta, can turn any situation into something positive. Wherever she goes, people can feel her positive energy. You get to choose to be around those who influence your decision-making and your mood, whether

SOURCE
1. https://www.nejm.org/doi/full/10.1056/NEJMsa0706154

through direct contact or otherwise. The OΣU encourages you to be choosy while building your support group. As you get more experience in playing the game, your support group may evolve as well. It is good to include positive books, podcasts, and other motivational constructive messaging as part of your support group.

III. DESIGNING YOUR "TO-BE" STATE FOR WORK OR BUSINESS

If you have a part-time or full-time job, you will dedicate anywhere from six to twelve hours a day to perform a set of activities related to it. Therefore, your choice in a job [or business] will impact your quality of life and level of personal satisfaction.

For many individuals, and depending on their current financial responsibilities, keeping or switching the way they make their income may be a tough decision. Many times, there is no need to make a drastic change in your environment or field of work. In some situations, changing one's perceptions and taking responsibility may be all that is needed to make a positive change in your work environment.

If you are unhappy and unsatisfied with your job or business, you won't be able to produce outstanding results. That is, if you are in a work situation that brings you down and makes you miserable, the most probable outcome is, you won't be performing at full potential.

Two individuals may have all the necessary skills required

for a job or business, but passion distinguishes one's happiness and satisfaction from the other. Our brain and subconscious mind become very creative when driven by passion. Anyone can develop brilliant ideas when engulfed by thoughts and emotions in line with their core vibrations. Having a passion for what you do as a job or business will reflect on the quality of your outcome and your level of commitment.

Before choosing to stay with your current career or switch paths, you must identify if you don't like what you're doing, in general, or if it's just that you don't love your current settings or environment. If you are a salesman, for example, and don't enjoy speaking to people, then the profession of selling might not be the correct one for you. However, if you love talking to people and like to help bring value to them or their businesses, but you hate the product you are selling, then perhaps selling a different product will solve the issue.

Sometimes you can face very challenging situations at your current job or in business. It can be overwhelming to notice the difference between letting go of the current settings and letting go of the field entirely. Following the guidance of the three A's helps in choosing the right path. If you don't like the outcome you are getting, no one else but you can change it. Ask yourself these questions, "Am I the best I can be at what I do for a living?" "Do I enjoy what I do?" "What can I do to bring more value to others?" Listen to your answers and pay attention to your emotions because they will tell you if you are on the best career path for you.

Training to be the best you can be in your job or business

requires continuous learning and putting new knowledge into practice. A person does not become the best in an area or career by doing nothing. Everything changes over time, and you need to evolve instead of allowing your mind to remain bound by a traditional way of doing things. Being good at something is the result of continuous learning. You can learn from experts, books, coworkers, clients, and every other source available to you in the field you work in. The outcome of your work reflects who you are. Giving your best efforts and maximizing your potential will increase your self-worth, confidence, and options.

If you find yourself with a constant lack of energy, no desire to give a little more than expected, no interest in learning new skills, or finding ways to make the job more efficient, you will find it very difficult to excel at what you do. In this case, you have some hard decisions to make. Either you move on and find another job, change your career path, or look for ways to make your current job more exciting. If these options are not feasible, you need to create a plan of action to build the path that would take you to your desired destination.

While formulating the new plan, there is another motivation technique to help alleviate the existing burden. This motivation would require redirecting your attention and energy, concentrating on the family, community, or anyone who benefits from the job's income. Focusing on areas outside work gives you a sense of gratitude and generates the positive energy necessary for formulating the new plan. Ideally, the new approach will incorporate the individual's passions and interests.

A. CHOOSE A CAREER PATH THAT CHALLENGES YOU

I.. YOUR SKILLS AND INTEREST

Do you have any friends or acquaintances that complain about one or more aspects of their job? Suppose the company you work for has political and cultural elements that are not in line with what you want. In that case, the responsible thing to do is to bring the issues up and propose solutions instead of complaining and gossiping. Complaining and being indecisive is immature behavior. If you are not happy with an aspect of your life, you need to do something to be part of the solution instead of adding to the problem.

You may want to own a business, be a doctor, lawyer, or cook. It does not matter the area of interest; what matters is that you choose SMART. What do I mean by "choose smart?" It means setting meaningful goals for yourself and setting the correct priorities for each one of them. In the end, you want to find a path that affords you to enjoy the journey. Life will be short for some and long for others; nobody knows what lies ahead. To achieve living in a stage of abundance, you need to combine short-term goals with long-term goals. A person who lives in misery their whole life, just to achieve a goal at the end, wouldn't be a very inspiring story to tell.

A goal that will only give you satisfaction after you achieve it [twenty or thirty years in the future] while living in constant pain, sadness, and unhappiness throughout the journey is simply not worth it, from my perspective.

2. BECOME THE BEST IN YOUR FIELD

Depending on your type of job or business, either part-time or full-time, you will most likely dedicate six to twelve hours a day to work. This is most of your waking time. So, the area you choose will significantly impact your quality of life and level of satisfaction.

During my career as a software developer, I worked in many different places, some better than others. There was a time I considered a career change to something completely different than what I was doing. I felt overwhelmed due to the incredible amount of work hours I accrued due to my overreaching objectives. Some were out of my control. However, I didn't take enough time for myself, not even to think and question my current situation. At the time, I blamed upper management because I saw them as the source for the mismanagement of the company's resources. One day I asked myself, "What am I doing?" I had crossed the line; I conflicted work with my number one priority; my family. How was I going to fix this situation? There was no point in blaming management, sales, or anyone else but me. I was the one who allowed those conflicts into my life. This situation taught me that I should not allow anyone to interfere with my top core priorities. The moment we compromise, we will develop a set of emotions that will drive us away from our objectives, creating an immense amount of stress.

The decision to either continue the journey or switch to

another one is always yours to make. At that time, maybe I put too much of myself on the line because I thought I was quitting instead of letting go if I left. Letting go of situations that cause you pain or interfere with your goals and life priorities is always the right thing to do; this is vastly different from quitting.

Quitting is dropping out due to fear or the lack of commitment and perseverance. To quit is to turn your back to a goal you would love to achieve but feel you can't do it because of weakness, apprehension, self-doubt, and unaccountability. The moment you take charge of your responsibility and ownership of the undesirable situation, you will realize what needs to be done to fix it. The most important thing you need to do to become the best you can be in your area of choice is to keep learning about it. There are many sources of vast knowledge and expertise. Combining expert knowledge and new knowledge will create the right balance for a creative brain

- Listen to audiobooks while driving or doing repetitive tasks.
- Read something about the latest research in your area of expertise at least once a week.
- Take courses related to your skills.
- As part of the morning routine, ask yourself, "What can I do today to perform my job better?"
- Think of ways to bring value to your customers and employees/employers.

If you don't train yourself to be the best you can be at your job, you will always be an average employee or employer. A person does not become the best in any area by doing nothing. There are processes and a set of habits that are at the root of success. First, there must be a flaming passion. Having a fervent desire will make you crave knowledge and open your mind to new possibilities. Everything changes over time. You need to evolve instead of keeping your mind fixed in the traditional way of doing things.

Knowledge is a crucial factor in keeping everything interesting. There is no way you will be a great asset in your area of specialization without continuous learning. If you don't want to learn your business-related skills, you may be on the wrong track. Therefore, you should find another way to make a profit. In this way, a first step can be to explore other possibilities until you discover something to feel excited about.

Becoming the best you can be at something is a journey that can make your life very enjoyable. You can lose your house, car, business, and all the cash you have saved, but the knowledge in your mind, the experiences, and the character you have built through them will be yours forever. No one can take it away.

The wrong environment should not stop you from wanting more and from becoming better at what you do. This is the only way to find a better position within a different environment or build another type of business.

Learning all the necessary skills needed to rise above average should be a must. Striving to become the best you can be in your area of choice can be very inspiring. You should always perform what is essential to succeed, and a bit more. Do not settle for average unless you are delighted at that stage. Based on my experience, it is worth going the extra mile to build character and internal growth. Once you experience the feelings and emotions that come from accomplishing something that requires this extra effort, you can decide based on these new facts if you feel happier now than before. Going the extra mile will most likely fulfill your life with more enjoyment and satisfaction as long as you keep aware of your decisions at all times.

GUIDELINE FIVE
TIME & KNOWLEDGE MANAGEMENT

I. TIME

Time is our most valuable resource. Most things can be bought, but no one can buy time. We have the same amount of time as the wealthiest person on the planet. The same twenty-four hours that make up a day is available to us just as it is to our favorite artist, the president or leader of any country, and any other person in the world. Time is a fair equalizer; it does not treat any one person differently. It does not favor anyone based on their financial or social status. Time is constant for everyone, and it will provide the same benefits or lack, depending on how we use it. To play the OΣU, I will ignore the theory of relativity from Einstein and other scientists and treat time as a constant of 24-hours for everyone, independent of where you live. Also, instead of using or wasting time, I encourage you to concentrate on investing in this amazing resource to get the most out of it.

Anyone who has written software knows that concentrating without being distracted is critical when developing new ideas and processes. The more you focus on something, the more in-depth your thoughts are. This enables you to see other ways to accomplish your objectives. Having distractions can be detrimental to your productivity, hence causing you to waste time. Phone calls, emails, and social media notifications create a lot of noise in your brains, making you lose focus on the task at hand. Enough time is available to achieve everything you want as long as you are disciplined enough to focus on a specific task for a predetermined amount of time without interruption. Otherwise, simple tasks like making appointments, organizing something at home or work, or researching a topic of interest, can all take double or triple the amount of time it should if you are inundated with distractions.

The Pomodoro technique suggests utilizing a twenty-five-minute interval on one task and then taking a break so your mind can recharge. This technique can help you if you are easily distracted. I find Pomodoro's technique helpful when I need to complete a task I'm not excited about, like organizing my closet or studying a topic that is not one of my favorites. However, to be productive in some tasks, you'll require more than twenty-five minutes. Still, this technique can be beneficial for administrative and social network-related tasks; it can keep you on track with time. The sense of achievement, self-content, accomplishment, and gratitude travels hand-in-hand with the use of your time.

We all have a set of activities we like to do when we

have free time. The way you utilize your time is a habit, like any other one. You may want to rest, watch TV for hours, or engage in sports activities. Some may instead choose to be with family and friends or engage in learning experiences. Others may choose to waste their time engaging in various harmful activities that may even be damaging to their health.

The lack of time is one of the most popular excuses utilized by those who don't want to take ownership of their lives. We all can invest time in ourselves, build relationships, acquire knowledge and experiences, and acquire the skill to improve a business or product. Taking cognizance of the importance that time gives us is an advantage because we start to invest instead of giving it for free to activities not worthy of our attention.

If you start making the best use of your time to gain knowledge, it will give you an advantage over those who accept ignorance as a virtue. People can be ignorant in an area because they do not have access to the information within or outside their area of interest. Understandably, we cannot have all the knowledge available from all fields. In other cases, some people choose to be ignorant by refusing to open their minds to objective and reliable sources of information. Ignorance in influential people makes them foolish and harmful to society.

It is easier to assess other people wasting their lives with meaningless activities than judging ourselves when we are the ones immersed in these affairs. This is because managing time is a habit. Spending a significant amount of time in front of your TV watching shows or news that make you angry or sad is an example of mismanaging your time. One of the worst things a person can do with their time is to use drugs or do anything that clouds their consciousness. If they are not aware of the decisions and actions during the time spent intoxicated, they may engage in unwanted behaviors. This will leave black holes or gaps in their chain of memories, generate regretful feelings and time wasted.

Lastly, another unproductive use of time is reliving painful memories of the past. The past is gone, and keeping your mind on reliving those experiences won't change the outcome and won't bring the time back. Rehashing the past will disable you from experiencing your present and building a better future.

On the contrary, engaging in constructive activities, like spending time with family and friends, will create more profound and meaningful relationships. Investing time in your job or business will ensure a brighter financial outcome. Investing your time in your inner self-growth will guarantee a life full of awareness and motivation. Committing time to help others will allow you to be part of inspiring quests you wouldn't otherwise experience. Investing time to grow in all these areas will ensure a balanced, joyful, and fulfilled life.

II. KNOWLEDGE

Knowledge is all the information, skills, and expertise you acquire through your experiences, learning from others' experiences, school, and other sources. The hunger for learning is a habit worth building. Knowledge opens your mind to new possibilities and ideas. You can learn in school and college from your experiences and the experiences of those who previously have been where you are now. The simple act of listening to people you admire and who motivate you will save you lots of time and effort. There are many books and great information from reliable sources on the internet. There are documentaries that bring years of experience and knowledge to your hands in a matter of hours or days. Our ancestors did not have the same opportunities to access as many learning sources as we do today. So, gathering as much accurate data and information as you can about your area of interest will put you in a position with a higher probability of success.

I encourage you to read about those who have prevailed or have failed in your field of study or expertise. There is an excellent opportunity to gain information and shortcuts when you learn about people thriving in your field or profession. There is also great value in understanding the causes and reasons why others have failed. Not knowing something will cause you to waste your most valuable resources, time, and physical and mental effort. You don't need to fill your mind with unnecessary information. Still, you should question and research anything available to your area of interest. Individuals that combine the knowledge available in books, documentaries, and other trustworthy sources of information, in addition to their own experiences, can prevent headaches and wasted time.

You should be mindful only to acquire useful knowledge that aligns with your goals, which will help open doors that lead you to your desired destination. In terms of social, political, news, and other generic types of data, be sure that your sources are accurate and based on facts. Otherwise, your mind will end up like a cabinet full of useless information.

Expending some time in understanding the foundation of a subject will build more significant benefits than only grasping superficial perceptions of a matter. For example, if you are making a dessert and think that it is not sweet enough, despite adding the right amount of sugar, you may add more sugar to make it sweeter. However, if you take the time to learn about the ingredients, you may have learned that salt helps to enhance the sweetness of a dish; adding a little salt will bring the dessert a perfect balance.

Though investing time to learn the principles of a subject will require a significant amount of time in the beginning, down the road, this process will become less time-consuming. Fundamental knowledge can be transferred from one area to another. In the example of the recipe, it would have helped to know how salt and sugar interact with each other would have enabled the creation of a more exquisite and exotic meal. The result would be long-lasting and the knowledge gained will be evident in every dessert subsequently prepared.

Learning focus principles about a business, a job, people, relationships, cultural differences, politics, and overall common sense prepares your mind to assess new knowledge or information more objectively. Your current results indicate the type of knowledge you care about and the information you allow to influence you. You need to be selective about this process.

Your body gets sick if you don't feed and take care of it

properly. The same happens with your mind. A mind without proper knowledge and information will be limited. Ignorance is usually harmful; it deters you from actualizing your goals. The state of an idle mind is worse than physical illness in many cases. Your body has tremendous physical strength when your mind believes it. If you make learning a habit, you will discover its power as a sustainable and reliable energy source and motivation. The thirst for knowledge and discovery will keep your body invigorated, and your mind will continuously generate new ideas. An active mind is a seed for an energetic and self-confident personality that will thrive to succeed.

Choose sources of information that are credible, reliable, and objective. News channels and social networks are all playing their own game, and their success depends on the number of users and followers they get. Ultimately, you decide who is worthy of your time and who you allow to influence your mind.

While I was working on my Masters in Information Systems at Stevens Institute of Technology, I learned something that stuck with me. In the beginning, I lost many points on different assignments, always for the same reason. One of my professors, Prof. Jerry Luftman, was very strict with the rules, especially when working on a research paper. He kept writing on my papers: "Be Specific." Research paper after research paper, I was in the same boat as many other students in the class. I would get big red circles in a couple of my paragraphs that read, "Be Specific." Some with an exclamation mark. After trying different approaches, without success, I decided to talk to him because I could not understand what he wanted. Upon talking with him, I finally got it. His message was, "Every statement on a research paper needed to be based on the specific facts. No feelings, no subjective comments; only information based on proof and supported by facts."

Going through that process created a sense of awareness, to date, of how valuable it is to understand the facts before making any decision and before communicating them. Once you get used to accepting information and knowledge based on facts, others won't be able to manipulate you. At the same time, you will be cautious about communicating conspiracy theories and misrepresenting realities.

Knowledge can shield you from false beliefs that result in unpleasant outcomes and immobilize you. It will protect you from being brainwashed. Enduring an unnecessary situation that causes you pain or disgrace to "tough it out" can be a misleading perception of persistence. The more knowledge you obtain from credible sources, the better prepared to identify where you need to be persistent. Being determined builds endurance and character that will help you tremendously to create the life you want. But believing and accepting unnecessary pain, suffering, and scarcity as assets to feel proud of should be unacceptable.

I was born and raised in the Dominican Republic, where the roles of females and males were very different. When a woman and a man indulged in the same act, they were judged differently by society. I remember always hearing unfaithful women being called "sluts" whereas an adulterous man's unfaithfulness is excused with comments such as, "yes, but he is a man." During a particular gathering, I overheard a conversation between some family and friends. I heard a beautiful young woman praising how lucky she was because, though her husband had an extra-marital relationship, he was still in their house. She felt like "the special one" because he had chosen her over his lover. To me, this was outrageous and unacceptable. I kept thinking, "*What kind of brainwashing power can someone have over another person, to not only justify this kind of behavior but to see it as an acceptable outcome, and to further inculcate in her the belief that she is the lucky one?*" It was a perfect example of how someone can take advantage of a person with low self-esteem and faulty beliefs, so they willingly become pawns to support other people's malicious games.

Ignorance is not bliss; it enables others to take advantage of you. Knowledge gives you power and increases your options. However, you must be sensitive to the ones who have no access to trustworthy sources of knowledge. There is a big difference between someone lacking access to expertise and reliable information and someone that chooses to be ignorant or stubborn just because of their ego or closed-minded mentality.

GUIDELINE SIX
TEN LIFE-CHANGING BELIEFS

LEADER APPROACH VS. HOPELESS ATTITUDE

With every goal you set and every lack of goal setting, one part of you is winning over the other, ensuring higher chances of that side winning the next time around. The more you allow gloomy thoughts, pessimistic beliefs, and negative relationships into your life, the more you become grim, hopeless, and a generally pessimistic person. However, the more you embrace your challenges, the higher the confidence to win and persist on the next.

One of the internal battles you may face when setting your goals is a conflict between the leader mindset and the hopeless mindset. For some, you may feel motivated, and your leadership forces take over, giving you energy and motivation. However, thoughts of doubt and lack of confidence will show up for others, and if you allow these dilemmas to take control, they will shatter or break your idea during its initial phase.

Your thoughts and emotions are usually within constant battle trying to win over determining your outcomes and pursuits. If the leader in you takes control, your chain of thoughts and actions will show motivation and energy, allowing you to be the best and happiest version of yourself. But if you let the slacker and hopeless side take control, you will generate negative thoughts and emotions, which will trigger actions that will take you away from the things you want. Images of defeat and fear would flood your mind causing you to falsely believe that you don't have what it takes to achieve your goals. An indefinite list of excuses will occupy every inch of you, and unless you shake it off, those negative thoughts and emotions will abort your idea before you take any action.

Let's go over ten common perceptions that will empower or hinder our character, depending on how we perceive them.

PERCEPTION I

HOPELESS ATTITUDE	LEADER'S APPROACH
"I don't have the resources I need."	"How can I make what I have work for me?"

During one of my trips to the Dominican Republic, I was with my family on a beach, enjoying the pleasant weather. As I was getting towels and sunblock out of a bag, a young boy approached and asked if there was anything my family or I needed that he could help with. We did not need anything; however, understanding the financial challenges many face in the Dominican Republic, I wanted to help him make some money, so I decided to ask him for something. I asked him if he knew where I"...could buy Limoncillo?" Limoncillo is a small exotic fruit found in the Dominican Republic that is very difficult to find in other places. He gave me a big smile while assuring me he would be right back with the fruit. Within fifteen minutes, he was back with two packages of a high-quality Limoncillo. He was a happy kid. I introduced him to my children, and they quickly bonded. He sat with us for lunch, we asked him about school and his parents. He told us he did not go to school most days because he needed to help his parents provide food for the rest of the family. He was only eight years old. He was very proud that he could help his family in some way. He also mentioned he loved the ocean and meeting people. He looked thrilled as he made waves with his feet on the clear water of Sosua beach. He was respectful and noble. This boy had a contagious positive attitude; he never showed any indication of sadness or suffering despite his run-down clothes, lack of shoes, and overall financial situation.

The encounter with that child was an experience of tenderness and humility. We witnessed how someone with so many financial deficiencies had managed to be resourceful and grateful for what he had at such a young age. This eight-year-old boy had already learned to create ways to help his family by brainstorming ideas for himself. His impact on us was so profound that my daughter wrote an article in his honor. The fact that all kids should have the opportunity to go to school instead of working at that age is another topic.

The lesson here is that you can improve your life regardless of the situation you are in today. Instead of complaining about your lack of resources, start by asking yourself, "What can I do today?" "Who am I?" and, "What do I have right now to improve my situation?" Your situation may be complicated, but posing that you don't have the resources needed can only cause people to empathize with you temporarily. But unfortunately, this will only encourage you to excuse your lack of action. It is not okay for you to feel powerless. The situation may seem harmless at first glance; still, it has the seed of impotence. This seed can influence you to give up before you make any decisions. Ingenuity and perseverance are necessary. You may not think you have all the resources you wish for today, but if you accept this perception as fact, you will never change your existence. If you can see it in your mind, then you have the tools to make it happen. Working with what you have available at this precise moment would start spinning the wheel in the direction you aspire. Find ways to discover solutions, create new paths, and use your imagination to open the door to the world you want. If you start your day asking yourself, "How can I improve...?" Maybe your attitude, physical posture, and behavior during the day will be very different than if you start by telling yourself that you don't have the resources to pursue a goal.

It is easier to hide your fears under cover of a lack of resources. Unfortunately, this attitude will get you nowhere. If you don't like where you are and think you can't take the first step due to a lack of resources, your future will look like your present or worse. Instead of complaining about things you don't have, focus on considering everything around you as a possibility. Your mind will begin birthing ideas or images of possible solutions. Every action you take gets you closer to the appropriate outcome. If you fall into deep waters and start thinking, "I wish I didn't fall." or "I wish I had a boat." or "I hope someone will come and get me out of this water." You might end up drowning. In such a case, the survival instinct should be to start swimming, even if you have not done it before. This automatic reaction happens when your subconscious mind takes over the situation. It's called fight or flight.

You don't need to wait until you are drowning to start swimming in life. If you don't like something about your life, don't blame others or the lack of resources. Ask yourself what you can do to make things better today. Is there something you can learn and become better at? Is there something you can do right now as the first step on your new journey?

Whenever we try something that doesn't work, we go one

step closer to the solution that will work. I have written a lot of code to build different software, and each time a version of such code does not work, I know I am getting closer to the perfect one. Yes, the process can be frustrating and overwhelming in some cases, but there is so much satisfaction when I finally get it to work that It makes it all worth it.

Using what you have doesn't mean constantly repeating an approach hoping that it will somehow give you a different result. Making yourself proficient in your current state of affairs allows you to evolve and adjust decisions when you don't get the intended outcome.

Our mind is our best ally when building our future. I don't believe that repeating phrases without making conscious actions will make things magically happen. But if we use our minds to set our intentions and keep our thoughts mindful of our purpose, we will notice that new ideas will keep coming up. Some may call these newly generated ideas messages from the subconscious mind, while others view them as answered prayers. It's okay to believe whatever makes you feel most comfortable as long as we acknowledge what we need to proceed with the appropriate course of actions generated from those ideas.

Believing that you can achieve a goal indicates that you have the tools necessary to make it a reality. Take action today. Take the first step without waiting for your current situation or environment to change. If you delay making your next move because of circumstances, you will waste time and lose motivation. Despite the number of struggles you are experiencing, either financially, socially, or relationship-wise, focusing on using your current capabilities will guarantee a much better future. Your tomorrow is defined by how you use the resources available to you now.

PERCEPTION 2

HOPELESS ATTITUDE	LEADER'S APPROACH
"No one supports me. I have not one."	"I am the sole Architect and Engineer of my life."

One of the primary purposes of the OΣU is to free you from your fears, excuses, and damaging past events. The fundamental way to achieve this is by following the three A's: Awareness, Action, and Accountability. You are responsible and accountable for where you are today and the person you will become tomorrow.

Maybe you were born into an awful condition. Perhaps you have negligent parents. Your upbringing could have been filled with all sorts of lacks. For some, lacking was financial resources or emotional stability. Or it may have been even more challenging if you lacked both in your upbringing. Everyone has a history that cannot be re-written. There may have been times in your life journey when you were in no position to make decisions or changes. Events and circumstances that you and your loved ones may have experienced while defenseless could have some lingering effects in your mind, generating negative emotions, fears, or a lack of confidence. Regardless of how bad or hard that part of your story is, you can always find someone who lived through worse circumstances and used those conditions to make a constructive difference in their life.

Others have decided to drift away from current detrimental events. Nonetheless, looking at your past as a training or learning experience and using it as a source of strength will give you the best results. Dwelling on the past will suppress opportunities to build a brighter future. Whatever happened is already done, so focus on how you want the next page in your book of life to be written.

Be sure to do your best to avoid being surrounded by pessimistic people often. It's OK to listen and try to help someone who is feeling down or frustrated from time to time. Still, if these individuals have a hopeless and chronic condition of negativism, and you realize they will never change, then it's better to minimize your exposure to them. Interacting continuously with people who don't believe in your ideas and who are always trying to impose their negative thoughts on you will eventually negatively affect your perceptions and ignite self-doubt. Once you start to doubt your ideas and goals, you begin to get away from them. So, you must limit the time you spend with pessimistic and unconstructive people.

If we wait until we get support and approval from others, we will be setting ourselves up for failure. Decide what you want and start moving towards it. If you don't find anyone that can support your ideas, books may become your best friend. You will discover brilliant partners willing to share their best pieces of advice from their years of experience. This is your life. You don't need permission or validation from others to strive for what you want in your heart. Build the design of your life malleable, so it matches your needs and wishes. We have all the approvals we need inside us. From now on, free yourself from anything that ties your wings, so you can fly as high in the direction you want.

PERCEPTION 3

HOPELESS ATTITUDE	LEADER'S APPROACH
"Money makes people bad."	"Money is an enabler that exposes who we are."

The belief that money makes people bad is prevalent in areas where there are many economic difficulties. Maybe these conflicting perceptions originated as a mechanism to give hope to people who otherwise felt no reason to believe in God and to eliminate questions about God concerning justice. Its origin may have been based on compassion to give some comfort to followers, but it is clear that it is a double-edged sword in the long run. The belief that God prefers poor people; that the kingdom of heaven is reserved for this group is misleading. Many people that believe money is bad also believe suffering is an asset. The misconception that all misfortunes and struggles an individual faces are signals sent by God is a cruel game that harms the impoverished and continues to control and bind their minds, hence creating more misery for them and their descendants. I believe that any form of God is not testing our endurance and faith through suffering. Someone with this firm belief loses their chances to become more financially stable for their own sake, their families, and society. It continues to create more scarcity by stopping individuals from believing in themselves and their sole power.

If a person is religious or a believer of any higher power,

they would have heard that "God" is full of love and forgiveness. As humans, we want to see our children and loved ones happy. If there is any form of God and that form is made up of pure love, then there would be no way that an entity of love could wish harm, scarcity, and suffering on their children.

Some individuals believe wealthier people are not trustworthy for several reasons. In most of these cases, these individuals are motivated by jealousy, envy, and dissatisfaction. While they praise themselves for being humble, the reality is, they lack motivation, leadership, and inner gratitude. Some wealthy people are mean, selfish, and self-centered and use their financial power to take advantage of others, but plenty of rich people have good hearts. It is not the money that makes them one way or the other; they would be the same way or have the same intentions if they had no financial assets. Money is not bad. Money is an enabler; it makes us more of what we already are. Some wealthy people use their financial freedom to satisfy their self-centered wishes, while others use some of their financial assets to help different areas of society. Each person is playing their own game and will perceive and use financial resources to amplify what's already in their hearts.

PERCEPTION 4

HOPELESS ATTITUDE	LEADER'S APPROACH
"I don't have time."	"I know how and where to invest my time."

Time is a valuable asset. No amount of money can add more hours in a day. We all have access to 24 hours each day and must maximize the use of these hours. Learning to manage time is a determining factor in the way we feel about ourselves and our outcomes.

Making the most of our time and effectiveness is essential to give full attention to the task we want to finish. Our brains work very efficiently, and when we give it a duty to perform, it will become very creative in coming up with ideas to resolve it. Depending on the task at hand, our thoughts will get into different layers of concentration.

If we need to develop innovations and critical detailed tasks, giving it our full attention will generate better and faster results. In most cases, the source of stress comes from mismanagement of time and spreading ourselves too thin among many tasks to which we cannot give the proper attention to each one.

Some activities like social media can quickly absorb our mind in our free time if we don't set some parameters. We only have 24 hours each day, and it is critical to make sure we make the best use of them. People who invest their time in constructive activities will have very different results from those who browse the internet with no purpose or spend the same time gossiping and generating inflammatory remarks.

The benefit of doing a task with purpose is not just to make that objective a reality; more importantly, it helps grow and transform our character. We become stronger in the process. The more experience we gain in practice, the better prepared we are to make better decisions in the future. Being purposeful in what we do gives our mind-muscle the exercise to build endurance and become more effective in overcoming more challenging tasks.

In the OΣU, we decide where and how to invest our time. Time becomes a strength or weakness, depending on our character and mind power. Everyone has access to the same amount of time in a day. Leaders manage their time differently than slackers do. We can use the time available to make things better and productive for us and others, or we can choose to waste it. Either way, the clock resets every 24 hours. With every new day, the previous day is closed and locked. We can do nothing about how we used our time yesterday or any day prior, but we have full power to manage our time today. Who do we want to be? Where do we want to go? The way we handle our time will determine the answers to these questions.

PERCEPTION 5

HOPELESS ATTITUDE	LEADER'S APPROACH
"Money only goes where there is money."	"I get more of what I set my Thoughts, Emotions, and Actions to."

It is easier for money to grow where the money is and for scarcity to increase where there is lack. Happiness will bring more joy, sadness will bring more sadness, anger will bring more anger, and so on. The mind plays a vital role in this process. An alcoholic will want more alcohol, so they strive to get it. A positive person will look for positivism and opportunities, so more positive things will happen for them. Some may see positive-minded people as lucky human beings. But there is no luck in this process; it is the logical result of the law of association and law of attraction.

Despite your goals and current circumstances in your life, it is always easier to attract more of what you have and what you believe in your mind. Your continuous thoughts create patterns that, through repetition, build habits. The idea that a person can see a glass half full or half empty is an outcome of the repetitive cycle of thoughts and emotions. You can only break this pattern by gaining awareness and practicing a new set of actions.

If negative people surround you, you will only be aware of adverse events. If your friends often complain about their kids, partners, or sickness, you will find that you may start complaining as well. Each one of us gravitates toward those similar to us. If you notice that you complain and feel gloomy most of the time, you should change your environment and spend more of your free time with constructive-minded people or engaging with constructive activities. After some interactions, you should notice that your perspective and perception of life have changed for the better. Books are always available and can provide excellent guidance and motivation.

If you want to attract something to your life, you must start thinking and gravitating towards that direction. This may mean breaking existing habits or existing rules. If a person never smokes, it is easier for them never to take a cigarette. On the contrary, if an individual is a smoker, it will take them some time and determination to break the association pattern between smoking and the pleasure they get from it. Money will flow easier within a person with mental wealth, just as happiness will bring more joy to a person with a mind of gratitude. If you find yourself on the opposite side of where you want to be, take this opportunity to find alternative paths to guide you in the direction you want.

In some cases, it's necessary to start with baby steps. If a person feels sad or angry all the time, it would be improbable to turn a switch that will change this person's perspective from one day to the next. But they can start improving their perspective, perhaps by lending a helping hand to someone, they don't know or giving to someone in need. There are many ways to help others using direct experience. This exercise seems simple but incredibly, and thankfully for us, it works wonders in building a positive mindset. This type of experience will trigger a sense of self-satisfaction that other incentives can not provide. The more you feel the emotions of self-satisfaction, the less sad or angry you will feel.

PERCEPTION 6

HOPELESS ATTITUDE	LEADER'S APPROACH
"I don't need or want anything."	"Being grateful does not mean to lack ambitions."

There is a big difference between being happy and pretending to be happy. Social media is over-saturated with posts by people who pretend to have everything going for them. All these posts can cause insecurities in others who feel lacking or insecure about themselves. The ones living in pretense try to ignore reality and make a bubble to shelter themselves within.

A happy person understands the facts and truth but chooses to face it by doing the best with the available resources they have. There is a lot of information on the subject of having a positive state of mind. But exactly how can one achieve that? How can one feel positive on a day that they are feeling terrible?

Having a positive mind and a constructive way of living does not mean turning a blind eye to reality. You should never live in a bubble, away from reality. Instead, having a constructive mind builds your character. It develops the habit of thinking positively to generate joy that will better prepare you to overcome any difficult situation you find in your path.

Suppose you plan to go hiking or go on a picnic and the weather changes from sunny and clear skies to rainy and cloudy. In that case, you can choose to complain the whole day about something out of your control, or you can adjust to the new reality and come up with a new set of plans to make the most of the rainy day. If you feel lousy with negative thoughts or self-doubt, you need to find ways to block this chain of those thoughts and emotions. There are multiple ways to achieve this, like watching a funny movie, reading funny jokes, listening to motivational speeches, or reading a good book. The point is to refocus your mind on constructive and positive thinking.

Being happy and fulfilled is very different from lacking ambitions—people who feel successful and accomplished set up goals and achieve them. The type of goal is not important because happiness is defined differently for each individual. But the motion generated by every achievement causes fulfillment and strengthens the personality of the individual. An ambitionless person lacks determination and professes to be happy to justify their lack of actions. They do not look for opportunities, and they believe that things will land on their laps. By claiming to be fine with what they have, they shield themselves from being seen as underachievers.

While living in the Dominican Republic, I was a doctor in Pharmacy. When I moved to the United States, I could not find any job related to my course of study, so I worked in a Check-Cashing business to make a living. During this time, I started my college validation. I worked up to 72 hours per week. I did everything required to excel at my job, including making coffee, sweeping the floors, and cleaning the bathroom and windows. Even though there isn't anything wrong with this type of work, these activities were not in line with my goals, especially after spending so many years with little sleep to get my pharmacist degree. I wanted other things. During that time, I kept having a recurring dream where I saw myself cleaning the floors and windows of the establishment while my colleagues and classmates passed by and laughed at me. I had a variation of this dream multiple times over the course of two weeks. The dream was the representation of my emotions and inner driving force guiding me in a different direction. These emotions pushed me to become aware of the numerous opportunities I could act upon. So I took drastic measures, and within 18 months, I completed an intensive computer programming certification that allowed me to get a job with a prestigious financial institution in New York, while getting my college validation at the same time. By then, I had found my passion for computer software and data. I chose my new path. Getting the college validation allowed me to get a master's degree two years after. I am not inferring that everyone should pursue higher education to find happiness. I encourage you to find and follow your passion.

If you pay attention to your emotions, you'll discover that they present indicators that show if your current path is the right one or not. You can feel these instincts as a sensation in your stomach or as a recurring thought and emotion; sometimes, they can come in the form of dreams. Everyone needs some quiet time for internal growth. There is so much noise and distraction around us every day. It can be challenging to set aside time and let your inner guide show the way. Connecting with your subconscious mind enables you to get a deeper understanding of who you really are. The habit of quieting our mind for a few minutes a day is one of the most efficient ways to feel the direction and understand our instincts.

The chances of completing a goal that will make you happy depend significantly on how well you know yourself. This means understanding your inner motivation, inner strengths, weaknesses, and, more importantly, the level of accountability you have about everything that happens in your life.

The 0ΣU is a game that a person with a hopeless attitude and lack of ambition will dislike because it pushes them beyond their comfort zone. There was a time in my life in which I believed I needed to accept everything without complaining. In my mind, I thought I just needed to deal with it using a passive mentality, even when I knew it wasn't good for me. Today I want to encourage you never to limit yourself to being a passive person. You should never compromise your priorities and goals to allow others to take advantage. More importantly, this is your game, and pretending to be anything you are not for the sake of what others may think wastes too much time, energy, and effort. Keep your focus on your priorities and targets.

PERCEPTION 7

HOPELESS ATTITUDE	LEADER'S APPROACH
"A job is a job; it is not supposed to be fun."	"What can I do to make my job more enjoyable?."

Many people don't like their jobs. They get up every morning to do something they hate, but they need the money. For some of us, switching a career path can be an option. But this can be a stressful dilemma for others. Working on something you like will give you many other benefits apart from monetary incentives. In general, adults spend most of their awake hours engaging in activities that generate economic stimulus, whether as an entrepreneur or an employee. As a rule of thumb, you should like your profession. It should give you a sense of progress and accomplishment. If someone dislikes their job, it would be challenging to feel overall happiness while spending so many hours engaging in meaningless and unpleasant activities. Ideally, you should work on something you love or, at least, like to some degree. This way, you will look forward to every day of work instead of anxiously anticipating retirement. Your job should keep you challenged and curious. If you hate your job, you must find something else. No amount of money is worth a life without enjoyment. Anyone that hates what they do for a living will find that happiness and self-fulfillment are impossible to achieve.

So how do you find enjoyment in what you do for a living? The first step is to understand if you dislike your job due to the environment (i.e., co-workers, bosses, or employees) or if the issue is more severe, meaning you don't like the required occupational duties. If a person is a cook and hates cooking, it does not matter how many changes occur in their environment; they won't find enjoyment. They could change jobs, employ other people, build a different restaurant, still, they won't be happy as a cook. Now suppose the cook enjoys cooking but has difficulties feeling a sense of accomplishment in their current setting. This auto inspection will enable them to see if there is something that can improve their perspective. In that case, they can objectively analyze if their perceptions are based on facts, emotions, or over-sensitivity. If they realize that the problem is the environment, then getting a job in another restaurant or opening their own restaurant may give them the satisfaction they need.

When you are unsure if your current career is the perfect fit for you, you can ask yourself these questions, "Do I enjoy the skills required as part of the main duties for my job?" "What can I do to make my job more enjoyable?" "What value can I add for my clients, users, and stakeholders, so I feel more engaged with my daily activities?." Notice these questions exclude any financial incentive. Money can sway your mind and create a temporary sense of happiness that, unfortunately, will dissipate as time progresses when other needs are not being filled.

Adding value, making existing processes easier for others, creating new ways to save time and money are usually good techniques to boost self-satisfaction at work. Your company, clients, users, management, or bosses are not responsible for you loving or hating your job. You have the power to decide, and you always have the freedom to change settings. Keep learning and continuing to build your knowledge portfolio. Knowledge is an asset that no one can take away from you. Also, it will differentiate you from others. Every time you become better at something, you feel better about yourself. The more you learn in an area of interest, the more inner eagerness you will produce to fuel your daily activities, decisions, and actions.

There is a tremendous advantage in inventing ways to work smarter rather than harder. Time is the most precious asset you have; the smarter you work, the more time you have for other things. Many people, when paying for a service, would rather pay for time than for value. Have you ever paid for incompetence? I have. We all like to think we don't pay for clumsiness. If your car breaks down and you call a company that sends a mechanic that you see working very hard for hours, how much would you tip them? I tend to give a good tip. Let's imagine that a few months later, the car breaks down again, and you call the same company, which sends a different mechanic. If the mechanic fixes the vehicle in 15-minutes this time, how much will you tip them? In this case, some people may give a much smaller gratuity because the mechanic made it look easy. The first mechanic most likely spent so many hours fixing the problem because he did not have enough experience or knowledge on how to do it. The second mechanic was an expert in the area, so he knew the solution right away. It is more natural to give a bigger tip to the person who seems to be working harder and longer than the expert who can do it much quicker. In this case, it's like we are paying for incompetence in the form of time. As we can see, there is no correlation between working hard long hours and the value of the outcome. Albert Einstein said, "The definition of genius is taking the complex and making it simple."

Everything is hard until you learn it. The only way to make something simple is to learn everything you can about it. With more knowledge, the easier it will be for you to build better solutions and magnify your options. The better you become, the more satisfying results you will experience, and the more free time you will get back to do other things.

PERCEPTION 8

HOPELESS ATTITUDE	LEADER'S APPROACH
"I will be happy when they change the way they are."	"I am responsible and accountable for my happiness."

If your happiness and self-fulfillment depend on others changing their behavior or personalities, you are positioned for failure. You cannot force anyone to change. Others can only change when they see the need themselves and decide to do it. You can influence their decisions, but ultimately, they too are playing their own game.

If you believe that everyone else is happier than you are, then it is true. Comparing yourself to others is a recipe for disaster. True happiness will always come from within. Nobody can buy true happiness with money. I must admit that financial tangibles greatly enhance external experiences of joy. Having financial stability minimizes stress and allows you to explore different lifestyles that enrich your inner happiness. If you feel that someone is happier than you, ask yourself, "What does that person have that I want?" If the answer is something tangible, you can set something similar as a goal for the next OΣU.

Physical things are easier to get than personal fulfillment, as the intangible emotion of continuous gratitude. For a person who feels happy and self-fulfilled, material things add to their physical adventures. If you don't feel mentally and emotionally satisfied and grateful, there is a big chance that you will pursue material things as a by-product. Setting tangible goals is good because they build the muscle of persistence and self-confidence. Additionally, you should continuously pursue internal growth to develop your inner strength and purpose.

If you are happy and feel fulfilled about your life, seeing your friends, family, and others become rich, wealthier, or more content will trigger joy within you. Gratitude enables you to celebrate when others win. A happy person wants everyone around them to feel accomplished as well. It is impossible to feel happy while envying someone else. People who feel serenity, contentment, self-fulfillment, and continuous gratitude will appear genuine and won't have to convince anyone about those feelings.

Everyone has unique tools to learn different things on their path. Gratitude and the happiness that comes from within is an internal growth process everyone can achieve at their own pace. It is a quest that cannot be forced onto others. If you intend to pursue your happiness, then start by avoiding comparing yourself to others. This race is only between you and yourself.

My father-in-law, Peter Antonini, is a philosophy professor and an avid golfer. He profoundly states, "When playing golf, you don't need to play against the other players; there is no actual gain in trying to beat your opponent. You can simply measure yourself against the course to achieve par, bogey, or even double-bogey." I love this quote because it is another reminder that we are the only one that matters and the only one who is worth competing against.

You should always keep going to great lengths to become better every time, not because of someone else, but because with every step further, you get stronger and fitter to take on more significant challenges that will give you the very best outcome in your life. I can not give you a formula for your happiness because this variable takes shape according to what truly matters in your heart. Practicing some silence and asking inner questions can start this process for you. You can take some time to think about these questions. "What is happiness for me" "What can I do to make my life more pleasant?" "What action can I take today that will enhance my positive state of mind?" "What changes can I make to feel happier and prouder about myself?" "What can I do to add value to the lives of others?" "What are the things I will be more satisfied with when I'm in my final moments?" Pondering over these questions will help open internal doors to mindfulness.

PERCEPTION 9

HOPELESS ATTITUDE	LEADER'S APPROACH
"I just can't do it."	"If I can see it in my mind, then I have the power to make it happen."

The idea that you don't have the "brains" to achieve an objective is usually a belief from fear or lower self-esteem. In many cases, the process of learning something new and challenging is like growing pains; It's not fun to go through the hassle but so worth it in the end. It takes determination and motivation. Once you have the encouragement, you will empower yourself with the necessary potential to learn and expand in every direction.

Do you know why a person stops their efforts before they have accomplished their goal? The main reason is self-doubt and the lack of believing they can do it. You have enormous power within yourself, you can call it anything you want, but the reality is, there is a strength within you that comes to the surface when you get out of your own way.

During one of my summer vacations, I was with my family at an all-inclusive hotel in the Dominican Republic. One mid-morning, I joined my family for breakfast. The breakfast was terrific. They had so many exotic fruits and fresh products, it felt like being in paradise. They had a variety of cheeses that looked amazing. I sampled many of the cheeses. They were delicious. At that moment, I was not aware that my body was developing an allergy to dairy. Right after breakfast, we headed to the beach. The weather was over 95 degrees. Before getting in the water,

I started having a heavy sensation in my chest. I was having difficulty breathing, and the feeling of compression on my chest kept increasing. I started heading toward my husband, and he noticed something was wrong. He held my arms, and we began to walk to the room where I had some steroid medicine my doctor had given me for similar issues. The path from the beach to our room was very long. By the time we got to the room, I couldn't even talk. I just took the pills, got inside an empty bathtub, and assumed the fetal position. Within thirty minutes or so, I began feeling better. I drank water, and my husband and I headed back to the beach to meet the rest of the family. On my way back, I noticed the pavement was burning hot; I walked on my tippy-toes. I asked my husband, "Did I walk this path without sandals?" I could not believe it.

The pavement was so hot that I developed full blisters on multiple areas of my feet. How did I walk that long path of burning hot pavement the first time without noticing that the pavement was there? This was possible because our minds have an incredible power just waiting for us to open its door. It shows up in times of desperate need, call it adrenaline rush or anything else, but the fact remains that our minds have the power to do logically improbable things when needed. When our conscious mind loses control in moments of emergency, the subconscious part of the brain and soul takes control and makes us do incredible things. For it, there is nothing impossible. It empowers us to push beyond our potential.

So how can you get access to this source of empowerment in your everyday, non-emergency situations? You need to have a target, and you need to believe in yourself with 100% trust. If you want something and set the proper goals and intentions, you will find a way to make it work. I am not talking of a desire, nice-to-have feeling, but the belief that you either get it or get it, without a single shred of doubt. The moment you allow your mind to see an exit, it will justify the lack of ideas. If you tell yourself that everything is possible and you genuinely believe it, then you will keep moving forward after every fall. If you try something and it doesn't work, you will try something else; like with software engineering, when a piece of code doesn't work, and we accept it as a fact, our creativity will shut down. However, if we don't give up and understand that there is a suitable solution just waiting for us to discover it, we will keep thinking and writing and thinking and rewriting code until we find the perfect one.

Anytime one method does not work, celebrate because you can check that method off the checklist. The more you fail, the closer you will get to the correct solution. If you are clear and determined to pursue your target, do not give up. Just keep trying different alternatives until you get it. Keep changing the approach, and eventually, you will find the one that works. You have all the power you need to make what you want a reality.

PERCEPTION 10

HOPELESS ATTITUDE	LEADER'S APPROACH
"I don't have the physique for this."	"I am proud of who I am. No one can be me."

There are many reasons why a person might not be happy

with the way they look. Beauty is relatively independent of the perceptions that have been built around the world. Skin colors of black, white, orange, and anything in between have the same value. If someone treats us differently because of our skin color, this only reflects a lack of maturity in their soul. Unfortunately, a person who treats people differently because of social differences results from internal issues and insecurities. Sometimes, this can be influenced by the wrong culture and misleading images in the media. These wrong perceptions are often rooted in some cultures and beliefs that hold tight to an old era. The reality is that under everyone's skin, there is a brain, a heart, and many organs working perfectly to keep us alive and make sure our bodies are executing to the best of their ability.

While studying pharmacy, some of my courses were held in the hospital of Santiago, in the Dominican Republic. One day, during one of my lab classes, there was a big commotion in the hospital. Many people were crying in the emergency room, and there were many police officers as well. I saw a person bleeding badly from the face while doctors were rushing him into an emergency room. I still remember his facial features clearly. His face had a big cut on the left side. There was a huge open wound. It started close to his nose, went across the side of his left cheek, and almost to his ear. I could see the ligaments, fat, and all blood coming out of his wound. There were people, maybe family members or friends, trying to start a fight. The situation was unclear, and I had no idea what was happening. This was a public hospital without the same restriction as a private hospital, so police officers had to get involved. As this took place in the emergency room, I noticed a few of my fellow classmates heading in the opposite direction. I decided to join them. Everyone was walking very fast. Soon after, I realized I was inside the morgue of the hospital. It was my first time visiting a morgue.

In contrast to the emergency room craziness, the morgue was super quiet; we could hear a pin drop. This time, I saw a body of a young skinny light-skinned male. He must have been in his mid-twenties to his early thirties. I got very close to him, a little bit in shock. There was no blood or bruises. His face looked like he was sleeping. My eyes started looking at his body, and on the top left of his chest, he had six or seven punctures. These cuts were just a little more than half an inch each. All of these cuts were the same shape and very close to each other. We could see the tissues and ligaments within the wounds, just like the person in the emergency room. The only difference was that this body had bled out, so there was not a single drop of blood coming out of his body. I realized I was staring at the body of the person who had just been killed by the individual I saw in the emergency room. That experience had a significant impact on my mind. These two men had different skin colors and body sizes. Seeing the cuts on both of them was like opening a window only covered by a thin layer of flesh. They both looked the same inside their bodies—a group of cells, tissues, and organs. Seeing a body that had bled to death was a similar sight to some other dead organisms. Our soul is what makes us unique, not the body.

We are all wrapped in different colors and textures. Under the covers, we are all the same in terms of physical value. Our spirit, character, and soul are what make us priceless. We are the only ones that can put a value on ourselves. The way we carry ourselves, value our lives and others, and treat ourselves and others increases or decreases our perceived value. Don't let anyone else tell you that you are not worth enough for whatever you are pursuing; such people are unhappy and uncomfortable within their skin. Making others feel bad gives them a temporary feeling of pleasure. They are arrogant to cover their weaknesses, acting with entitlement, and pretending to be better. They feel falsely superior to others as a result.

The more you learn, the more you execute, the more you become. This cannot be seen or measured based on what you have (tangible things) but by who you become—the you that no one can steal and manipulate. You are the only one that can experience the pleasure of being yourself. No one can buy your uniqueness, your strength, your experiences, and your wisdom. It has priceless value. Self-confidence is the highest attractive power. A decorated image can make a person feel exceptional, but such height will not be permanent without a solid foundation and high self-esteem.

GUIDELINE SEVEN
FAITH

Faith is a firm belief and trust in someone or something. This feeling is subjective to each person. Faith can have a positive or negative effect when you play the OΣU. It is a powerful belief that will significantly impact the Thoughts ➤ Emotions ➤ Actions cycle. The combined forces of doing everything you can for a goal and putting your faith in God or any other superpower to help you achieve your goal can make you more confident in yourself. It may give you a greater sense of satisfaction during your journey. On the other hand, if you do not carry out any action and maintain a passive behavior, thinking that a God or superpower will take care of everything for you is wishful thinking.

A few years ago, I had to consult an oncologist because a very dear relative was predicted to potentially develop a hazardous type of cancer. I had the opportunity to meet with one of the best oncologists in the United States. He is very respected and prestigious in his field. He has a long list of success stories of helping individuals with various types of cancer. During one of my visits to his office, I noticed several teenagers and young adults with amputated limbs. Whenever I saw a teenager come to his office, I felt a knot in my stomach because I knew the unsettled situations they and their parents were going through. It was as if I could feel the pain and sadness of those parents.

This doctor was very upbeat and energetic and made us feel confident that we were in the right place. During one of my conversations with him, I shared that I was impressed by his positive attitude despite dealing with so many painful and sad cases. I was stunned by how humble and calming he was. He told me that there are situations that even he, with all his experience and studies, could not explain with science. According to his anecdote, there were occasions when only a miracle could explain his patient's recovery. Listening to him speak that way made me examine my personal beliefs. As I heard him say the word "miracle" as the only way to explain someone's healing, despite the science determining odds, brought to light another meaning of the word faith.

I have personal opinions and experiences that cannot be explained by science either. But could this mean that we just don't have enough data yet? Could science explain these inexplicable experiences some years in the future? Are the miraculous events in our times the results of wonders or natural outcomes from sources we are not aware of yet? Could science and faith be intertwined? These are thoughts I ponder over as I think about the relationship between science and faith.

My dear friend, Andrew Wilson, is a very talented software engineer and a great human being. He is an atheist, meaning he does not believe in a higher power or God. He describes what others believe as miracles as, "Scientific reasoning is used to find the truth, the absence of truth is not falsehood, the absence of truth is the unknown. Miracles are the unknown. It's better to wait for the truth to reveal itself rather than risk believing a falsehood." His perspective and that of the doctor, a person who believes in miracles and faith, are very different. Nonetheless, each outlook acknowledges that there is an "unknown" that manifests itself and isn't always explicable through science.

Many years ago, I met a very humble woman at the gym who was a cancer survivor. She signed up to work on building up her muscles after winning the "big fight against cancer." She was a fervent believer, one of the most religious people I have ever known. One day she told me her story about her cancer diagnosis and how eventually she was sent home to die. Her doctors concluded that there was nothing else they could do for her. So, she prayed and had other groups praying for her. She told me that she had a dream that felt more like an out-of-body experience one night. In this dream, she told me, she was "surrounded by doctors who performed some type of surgery on me. There was a lot of bright light surrounding the doctors." She continued her story, saying that "in the morning when I woke up, I was able to get up from my bed and eat." Something she hadn't done for days. So, she went back to her doctors, and according to her, "they were shocked to see me alive." They performed another set of tests on her, and this time there was no sign of the cancerous tumor. She believes the cure of her cancer was a true miracle from God. I saw her again after about 15 years, and she is still healthy and a faithful believer in God.

Are either the believer or non-believer's points of view right or wrong? Some of the answers to the unknown we see today may not come during my lifetime or yours. Maybe the answers to these questions will be related to energy, light, or some other form of god or higher power, or perhaps there will be a scientific explanation for them. Independent of this, there is a reality: when people believe in the impossible, the probability of attaining the most promising results is most likely to happen. For some, having active faith when playing the OΣU will increase their chances of achieving their goal when facing extreme challenges. This feeling will keep them motivated and assertive when they feel defeated. For others, taking actions into their own hands and believing solely in themselves will be the answer to achieving their goals.

No one can or should impose faith on anyone. If a person

is an atheist, it will take a "miraculous" experience for this belief to be born within themselves. Meanwhile, if a person is a believer, they will see miracles in everything. Each person should use all of the tools available to them and anything they believe will make them more powerful and confident. Faith or no faith does not make any person good or bad, but instead, the actions and the way believers and non-believers behave towards themselves and others make the real difference in their life and the results of their 0ΣU.

GUIDELINE EIGHT
LIVE A LIFE WITHOUT REGRETS

If you have ever competed, you'll know that there are times you win and other times you lose. It is reasonable to feel disappointed after losing in any competition. Not everyone that fails in a tournament feels the same way. Some feel unhappy with the outcome but feel proud of their efforts, while others may feel discouraged and full of regrets. It all goes back to how much you give of yourself to the task at hand. Did you prepare and train as much as you could, or did you train halfway? When you commit one hundred percent to everything you do, your spirit, character, and confidence get stronger and better prepared for the next challenge. This process transforms your body and mind constructively, independent of the outcome. You know, if you give everything you can, there will be no regrets. Meanwhile, suppose you don't get your desired result due to a lack of discipline and effort. In that case, the feeling of weakness and incompetence will be reinforced, which will continue to negatively affect all other areas of your life.

There are two growth areas for each goal you set; the body and mind. They need to be trained in parallel. If you are trying to play a sport, you need to practice, build muscle and endurance. If your goal involves studies or business, you need to learn as much as possible and develop the discipline required to execute all the necessary actions.

Everything you do and everything you pursue needs to start from your mind. Taking the time to strengthen your mind will pay high dividends. A sense full of confidence and motivation can push the body to the hardest and longer distances. You become a different person in the process. More importantly, your mind is like any other muscle. The more you train it with constructive reassurance and positive beliefs, the more it will expand to show you more possibilities and opportunities all around you. The mind must reach the goal before the physical body. A strong belief in oneself has a strong effect on the outcome. With every success, you achieve, the higher likelihood of achieving more in the future. If you have missed a target, don't feel disappointed. A failure is a single event that is not a reflection of who you are.

The 'Σ' symbol of the OΣU is a reminder that we are the sum of all the pieces and parts that compose who we are. Winning or losing a single event represents a minor component of this complex universe within us, but building a winner vs. loser mindset is a trait that affects every other element that forms our total sum.

Make a habit of always doing the best you can while being aware of your present state of mind. That is one of the secrets to living a life with no regrets. Some people live in a constant stage of depression or sadness, and at times, they don't even understand the cause. Some depression results from a medical condition, so anyone experiencing depression should always consult a doctor. However, the fact remains, our minds have a tremendous impact on the way we feel. The feelings of regret can be very hard on an individual because it is usually accompanied by feelings of helplessness and a need for a do-over.

We often encounter people who have lost a loved one and wish they could see them again. They may say things like, "If I could see my mother again, I'd ask her for forgiveness." or "If only I had more time to show how much I love them." They resent the past because they recognize they failed in their actions. If our loved one is not with us anymore, then it is too late to repair the damage. The only way to heal at this point is by recognizing the fault and forgiving oneself. This is the first step to moving forward. I am sure your loved one would be happy to see their family moving forward with your lives. Living a life with no regrets means being aware and observant of your decisions and actions.

Let's say an individual goes to a party or business event, and someone with authority or popularity offers them drugs that they accept and use as a way to fit in. Once they are under the drug's effects, their behavior changes and actions are different from how they normally conduct themselves. The next day they're woken up by a phone call asking if they have seen the video circulating on social media. Of course, they do not have an idea of what happened. To their surprise and embarrassment, the video is about their unimaginable poor behavior. In this situation, the individual will experience tremendous guilt and regret. However, if someone consciously decides to use drugs or any other product that will cloud their mind and decision-making, knowing full well of the consequences, there would be no regrets when a video of their irresponsible behavior begins to circulate. They took the risk knowing this could be a possible outcome.

As you can see, it's not the outcome that determines the level of regrets in a person's mind but the level of awareness and consciousness involved in the decision-making process. The OΣU only concentrates on the present and the future because the past no longer matters. Many individuals feel angry, unhappy, and lack motivation because they focus on the history, recalling memories of pain and undesired results. No one can turn back the clock. Whatever happened, and for whichever reason occurred, it is already over. Holding on to the past can become a black hole in your soul that keeps sucking in the present and sabotaging your future until you let it go. Use your energy on the things you control and start living to the fullest in the present with an anticipation of a brighter future.

Many teenagers go through a phase of craving to fit in and be "liked" by their peers. In the process, many times, there is a loss of identity and authenticity. This loss can be temporary or permanent. Going through this process at an early age can be a standard growing mechanism for building their character.

However, it becomes a significant weakness if this identity loss continues during adulthood.

It is best to determine if your actions during your day-to-day activities align with your inner being or if you are only doing things so people will like you. You don't need approval from others to pursue your dreams. Once you grasp and own who you are, you begin to acquire a different type of energy. This energy is an unlimited power source that will keep you charged 100% of the time because it is self-sustainable. When you execute actions that go against your soul's interest just because you want to fit in, the conflict between these actions and the core of who you are will create a clash and unbalanced set of emotions. The activities executed, only to fit in or be liked, result in a short span of happiness, then is often followed by a more extensive span of sadness or depression. There is no need to fit in when you behave authentically. Your authenticity naturally gravitates you toward a circle of people and circumstances with similar synergies. Once you own who you are, you will feel no need to be "liked" by others because you will be self-content within your skin. Keep in mind that when you strive to be liked by others, you voluntarily allow them to affect your game, often leading to a negative outcome. Everyone is playing their own game. What do you benefit from empowering others to make you feel vulnerable for the wrong reasons?

The 0ΣU is all on you. Managing your social presence, your inner circle, and anything that can affect your mind is your choice. You control every move and decision within your game. You decide how much value it brings you and at what cost. You go through the T.E.A. loop multiple times daily.

It goes like this:

This infinitive loop is part of everyone's game. The more you master how to trigger and change this loop, the higher benefits you will see propagate to all areas of your lives. Managing the T.E.A. loop will enable you to understand who you are and show you areas for self-improvement that will help you attain your goals faster. It will provide a sense of freedom and a sustainable inner source of power.

GUIDELINE NINE
ENABLE POSITIVE ENERGY TO FLOW IN YOUR SPACE

A few years ago, we decided to buy a new home. We started looking for options on the internet and visiting neighborhoods we were interested in. Sometimes we drove by excellent locations imagining how the houses would look inside. We became experts in going to open houses, and we got a better idea of what we wanted in our new home and the things we wanted to stay away from. I remember one of the houses we saw; it was beautiful. It had a wonderful yard and many windows so we could see it from the outside. It looked perfect. There was an open house coming up that weekend, so we made sure we were one of the first to arrive. The owners were still in the house, though getting ready to step out, and we had the chance to meet them. At the entrance, everything looked great. There was plenty of light and open space. It was evident that the floor had recently been remodeled. It was spotless. The floors were a combination of tiles and hardwood. They clearly took time and invested money to come up with the design. That first impression didn't last very long. As we moved to the other rooms, the number of things cluttering the spaces kept growing. There were several pairs of shoes in one of the bedrooms. There was dust all over. It wasn't easy to switch our attention to anything else. The smell of humidity and staleness invaded the atmosphere. We went through the various rooms and eventually ended up in the basement. Soon after, I began to feel claustrophobic. This sensation was not due to the lack of windows or doors; it was due to all the clutter blocking the windows and doors.

Many curtains and items were hanging on the wall. A host of comforters and pillows in excess were all over. I tried to keep my posture, and then I politely told them I wanted to see more of the upstairs. In all honesty, I just needed to get out of that space. Eventually, we headed toward the main entrance. I complimented the work they had done at the entrance. That was the only part of the house that was uncluttered and clean. Despite the house having a good layout, it felt very uncomfortable to be inside. It felt so "heavy" that I couldn't wait to get out.

Over time, the house failed to sell. It was put on the market twice, and each time it was subsequently taken off. The reason was apparent to me; there was too much clutter and dust that energy and sunlight could not flow through the home. Most likely, all possible buyers felt the negativity and heaviness of the house's atmosphere, and I imagine that was the main reason the house did not sell.

Organizing and cleaning our space is an essential task everyone can achieve. Decluttering is very important to allow the energy to flow in our whole environment. You will feel much better right away after getting rid of the stuff you don't need.

Have you visited a place that feels awkward, although what was visible in the environment seems to be in order? This often occurs when all the closets and other areas are filled with many things that are not in use. You should not hide your clutter in closets, under the bed, or in other hidden spaces. It is best to declutter to bring balance and energy flow to your home, not impress friends and other visitors. If you are not used to having your space organized, it is possible you do not realize the trails you have formed around you. It is also possible you do not realize how heavy it is in the atmosphere you live in. But don't worry, soon you will see and feel the difference once the environment is cleared.

The first phase of decluttering can be overwhelming. This starts with emptying closets, boxes, cabinets, furniture, and every other occupied space. Once everything is out, your place will look like a bomb went off. You will feel overwhelmed at this point. You may have the urge or sensation to get out of the house. You will want to do just about anything that will distract you from facing the task at hand.

As daunting as decluttering may seem, you should be involved in this process, even if you pay others to help. You can pay someone to declutter your house, but they can't get rid of the things that are of no value to you without your guidance. It is best not to try to declutter your entire home all at once. It is more manageable to choose one room at a time. If the room is large and has too much clutter, you can start by picking one area. To make this process successful, you should spend at least thirty minutes every day getting rid of all the things you don't use and don't need until your space is clear for good energy to flow.

It is vital to pay special attention to every item in your home. Everything you look at should bring you joy, or at least it should not give you any negative memory or emotion. It is better to take everything out from time to time and then add one item back at a time. This will help to bring focus to your area. Remember, the objective is not for the place to look clean and organized but for the place to be truly clean and organized. Closets can become very messy very fast. It is essential to bring harmony to your closets. Every day you look at your wardrobe for one reason or another. It feels enjoyable when it is organized. You may like to arrange by colors while others might prefer to arrange it by occasion. It is entirely up to you. The important thing is that when you open your closet, it looks taken care of.

You should get rid of any item you don't love, even if it is a gift. If you look at an item that makes you feel uncomfortable, you need to remove it. If there are pieces in your closet that you ignore and push aside, then get rid of them. If you haven't used a piece of clothing within the past two years, this is an excellent indication you don't need it. Perhaps you keep your shoes in the same closet as your clothes; make sure to clean their bottoms frequently. You must avoid bringing the dirt and energies from the outside into your sanctuary, which is a very intimate part of your life. Dirty clothes should have their own place separated from the clean ones. Refrain from piling your dirty clothes in the corner; instead, place them in a container or designated area. Your possessions and the clothing you wear carry your energy. If I have a bad day, I make sure I clean the clothes I wore that day. If they need to be dry cleaned or very delicate and I don't want to wash them, I let them breathe under the sun and air.

You should keep the space under your sleeping area completely clean and decluttered. We spend a significant amount of time over in our beds, so making sure the energy flows freely is vital. In addition to keeping the area under your bed clear of clutter, I find it super helpful to make the bed every day. If you are not used to doing this, you may find it unnecessary and a waste of time, but give it a try. This process somehow helps with how you start your day and how you finish your day. My husband used to say, "Why do it in the morning if I am going to use it at night, and it will be messy again?!" Over time he began to notice the difference it made with having a made-up bed. I was pleasantly surprised to find him making the bed whenever I forgot or was in a rush. Here is the thing, you will feel better and more energized during the day if you declutter and make your bed.

If you feel upset or puzzled about something, I suggest taking a head-to-toe shower while allowing yourself to think about nothing. If you cannot keep your mind clear while in the shower, imagine your body surrounded by a light, cleaning all the negativity around and within. Ideally, everything you see in your house should give you content. Nothing within your home should breed negativity or make you uncomfortable when you see it or pass by it. I love plants and pets to brighten the atmosphere and bring life to a home. It is best to listen to your feelings and follow according to the emotions you feel.

Finally, keeping everything clean is a wonderful way to keep the energy moving. Once everything is clean, I like to burn incense, sage, or any fragrance that calls my attention. Additionally, oils like lavender and lemon-grass create an aroma that creates a very relaxing atmosphere that is calming for me. There are so many oils and fragrances to choose from. Find one that you like and feel resonates with you.

Energy needs to flow throughout your home to bring balance, and when that happens, you'll feel balanced.

PLAYING THE OΣU THE 63-DAYS CHALLENGE VS. THE SHORT VERSION

The OΣU short version consists of playing one week while targeting a smaller short-term goal. Committing to one week creates an opportunity to see some of the benefits of this game with a short commitment. A week is not enough time to build a habit or to change an existing one. Because of this factor, this short version is meant to start a quick routine that will exhibit some results, especially in your state of mind. Playing for a week should help lower your stress level while experiencing higher concentration and inner motivation. Furthermore, it will show benefits on relationships, quality, and productivity in your work or business, and it should spark some internal questions and more profound feelings.

The full version involves challenging yourself through a 63-day program and consciously actively playing your zero-sum game. This version will incorporate the benefits of the short version but on a larger and deeper scale. While taking this challenge, there will be a clear picture of your most important targets and a clear understanding of the cost associated with the gain concerning your priorities. By the end of the 63-day program, you would have built the new habits necessary for your action plan. You should experience more mental clarity and a sense of purpose. You will feel more in control of your destiny and empowered to continue building your life while keeping your inner negative, hopeless side in check, so the leader side of you can continue winning its game.

The 63-day program will free you from existing unconstructive habits, opposing cultures, damaging beliefs, and hopeless thoughts. Therefore, getting rid of all emotions that do not align with the goals you want to accomplish while guiding you in balance with your core priorities. It will enable you to feel what decisions are correct to execute. This challenge will allow you to connect with and understand your subconscious' messages. This process will open the door for inner discovery while increasing your consciousness and positive outlook. Taking this challenge will provide you with the necessary tools to achieve the things you want.

Only you can benefit from this experience, and the results for everyone may be very different. Still, there is a shared benefit; everyone who plays this game should be happier with a greater sense of purpose and gratitude, high self-confidence and motivation, and some meaningful accomplished successes by the end of the 63-days. More importantly, you will have created a solid foundation for achieving major long-term dreams.

THE 63-DAY PROGRAM

According to many studies, a person needs 18 to 254 days to build a new habit. Many suggest that 21-days is enough to do so. I've tested the theory of building a habit in 21-days, and based on my experience, 21-days was not enough to create a habit I could perform in auto mode. The OΣU recommends using these techniques and exercises for nine weeks, making the whole program 63-days. The reason for nine weeks relates to the metaphysical meaning of the number nine and its relation with compassion and awareness, among other sacred geometry meanings. Committing to playing the 63-day game will increase your chances immensely to build new habits, get rid of unwanted ones, and achieve a level of awareness that is difficult to achieve otherwise. 63-days (9-weeks) is enough time for most people to build new habits, discard negative ones, and establish a proper set of action plans to achieve their targets.

You will begin to see some benefits before ending the program. Depending on how long and deep the roots of existing habits are, the process to get rid of them completely might take a little longer. Just stick to it until you find yourself executing the newly created effective practices on auto-mode. After 21 consecutive days, it will get more comfortable for you to perform these new activities. You will be able to measure your progress by the level of energy, motivation, awareness, and sense of freedom, responsibility, and confidence you have. By the end of this program, you should feel optimistic about the future, and by then, you should have seen the outcome of obtaining a few short-term goals and the foundation for longer and more challenging ones.

During these 63-days, you will learn to manage your thoughts and emotions to trigger the correct set of activities to attain your targets. You should start seeing results by the first week of doing these exercises. With each repetition, you will be reinforcing your new way of thinking and the new way to channel your emotions. Some common goals can be attained within a couple of days or weeks as a test. Some examples are, improved relationships, feeling better about your job or business, improved decision-making, and increasing energy and motivation. But even after you achieve a short-term goal, if you don't continue building the habit of creating a positive chain of thoughts and emotions, your actions will revert to your old way of doing things.

The $0\Sigma U$ does not judge a goal or objective to be fair, just, improper, or wrong. If you use these techniques, you will attain your goals, irrespective of what they are. To successfully win this game, you need to complete all actions full of awareness and no regrets. To help achieve this, there are bonus points for those who decide to engage in tasks that involve helping others. The bonus activities are designed to plant the seed of gratitude and personal satisfaction, which are difficult to experience for someone unfamiliar with them. You will concentrate on generating a specific set of emotions from intangibles, ensuring that you can enjoy the journey, and ensuring that there will be minimal to no regrets by the end of the game. As with any other decision you make while playing the $0\Sigma U$, it will be up to you to take the challenge of earning the bonus points or not.

The initial phase of playing this game, or level one, is to create the foundation which you will use as a core structure to support all of your journeys. All of the examples used as a baseline for the game are portraits of the leading forces within you.

Levels 1-3 three consist of solving the enigma of what constitutes the meaning of happiness and addressing the core values that make you who you are and who you want to be. Additionally, they include the tangibles and intangibles benefits. By completing these levels, you will have fundamental core knowledge about who you are, what you want, and the price you are willing to pay for your targets. You will have a great understanding of your passion, core priorities, and what you want in the short and long term.

At the end of this chapter, you will find the OΣU Cheatsheet to give you a summary and quick way to checkpoint your progress during the 63-days program. Each area has different activities and number of points associated with them. You will find these four core areas.

» Morning Routine - 2 pts
» DaytimeCheckpoints - 5 pts
» Evening Routine -2 pts
» The protector - 1pt
   ** To be used against the hopeless part in you. In addition, the protector has a special key to opening doors of happiness, fulfillment, and gratitude.

By the end of this chapter, you will learn all the activities related to each one of these areas and how to track if the leader or the hopeless part in you wins the game

THE OΣU LEVEL I
YOUR PASSION

———————————

Take ten cards or pieces of paper and write the title as you see in figure A. Take your time and write as much information as you can on each one of them. The combination of knowing what you love, like, dislike and hate, and the things you are good and bad at will give you an excellent understanding of your talents, instincts, and the things you most enjoy doing

FIGURE A

List the things you love to do	List the things you are good at	List topics that interest you
List the things you don't like doing	List topics that don't interest you	List the things you don't like about others
List the things you are good at based on objective facts	List the things you admire about others	List the things you are grateful for

If money and time were not a constraint, what Is the one thing you would do within these three categories:

» Yourself
» Your loved ones
» Others or a cause you care about

After you are done identifying your passion, take these cards and put them in a place you can go back to review them multiple times during the day. Update them with more information that comes to your mind. At night before going to sleep, take a look at them one more time. Then clear your mind and fall asleep, letting the inner you gather some answers overnight. In the morning, take the cards with your notes and, without judging, make any adjustments following your feelings.

You can repeat this process a few times until you feel the excitement in your chest about discovering your passion and purpose. Once you feel these emotions, you can move on to level two.

THE OΣU - LEVEL 2
YOUR PRIORITIES

Level two is a variable, meaning it can change according to your age or what phase of life you're currently in. To understand your priorities, you must free up your mind of any lingering thoughts about others. Depending on your upbringing, there might be conflicts in your mind between the things that are really important to you vs. the things that have to do with others because you feel guilt, and you believe others should be the priority instead. This is your game, and no one can make you feel that something should be a priority unless it truly adds value to the quality of your life, something that will be devastating for you if you lose it.

Remember, you are designing and engineering your life to the way it has worth, meaning, and satisfying for you. So you must take the time to identify the most critical things in your life.

Now, take ten cards or pieces of paper and write the title as you see in Figure B. If you have a priority that does not belong to any of the categories suggested in Figure B, please feel free to use the ones applicable to you. Take your time to write as much information on each of them. Once you are done writing each priority in a separate card, go back and assign a ranking in ascending order. Your highest priority should be identified by #1, followed by your second priority with #2, and so on. Concentrate on your top three priorities. They will have a significant impact when moving to the goal-setting level.

FIGURE B

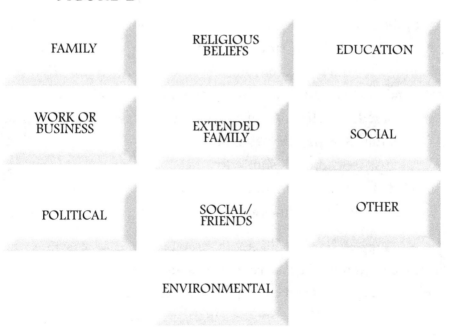

FAMILY	RELIGIOUS BELIEFS	EDUCATION
WORK OR BUSINESS	EXTENDED FAMILY	SOCIAL
POLITICAL	SOCIAL/ FRIENDS	OTHER
	ENVIRONMENTAL	

Understanding the value of each of your top priorities is critical. Pursuing goals that compromise priorities that rank from 4th–10th is a very different predicament than compromising your top three priorities. There is a strong correlation between compromising any of the top three priorities and experiencing feelings for regrets. Since you know there is no way to override history, it is best to take the time to define these priorities with the proper rating. Once you feel confident in understanding each of your core priorities, you can move to level three

THE OΣU - LEVEL 3
SET YOUR GOALS

Setting up a destination is what makes the journey enjoyable. Having a purpose is the fuel that will keep you moving in the good and hard times. Without an intention, anyone can manipulate your mind and make you more susceptible to their demands. When you obtain an objective, which you have planned and worked to achieve, you will feel a unique emotion and a success that will increase your self-esteem and confidence. This emotion will encourage similar feelings, significantly increasing the probability that you will continue achieving more meaningful goals in all areas of your life.

Suppose you think about previous experiences in your life, where you worked and achieved a goal, and compare them to other times you got something you wanted as a gift. Even though a gift will bring the feeling of delight, receiving something you did not work for won't have the same impact on your character as working and earning would. When you decide to achieve a goal, a new set of energies start developing in your body and mind. When you work toward a goal, your mind-muscle is being trained. In working towards achieving an objective, there are changes in your disposition and mind. The reward of overcoming each difficulty is wisdom and strength that you can not buy with any currency. If you follow the three A's of the OΣU - Awareness, Actions, and Accountability, then you'll celebrate when facing a new challenge. This indicates that you are moving forward. With each milestone, your character and personality continue to evolve into a sounder and more confident version of yourself.

You can use Figure C as guidance for setting up goals. The section on bonus goal choices is highly recommended. The purpose of the bonus goals is to open the door for you to experience gratitude's wonders.

FIGURE C

House	Business	Education
City, country, price of the house, neighborhood, interior settings.	Type of business. Product or service. Determine value to customers. Expected income.	Degree. Training. Empiric knowledge. Define source of education.

Partner/Mate	Work	Vehicle
Type of partner. Their core values. Other details important to you.	Type of company. Define expected income and other benefits. Define job activities.	Define type of car. Model. Year. Color. Safety features.

Family	Financial Stability	Financial Freedom
Define desired relationships.	Define total desired amount and when you want to achieve specific amounts.	Subjective to desired life-style. Define the specifics to your desire.

THE OΣU - LEVEL 4
ALIGNING OUR GOALS WITH YOUR TOP PRIORITIES

All the information you need to define your short-term and long-term goals is within the cards in the three prior levels. Your passion shows all the things you enjoy most. Therefore you will be able to execute them with pleasure and enjoyment even when there are difficulties. Your goals are the tangible and intangible things you want to attain. Maybe you need to have that goal in your life now, perhaps not. If you feel you must have it, you will be charged with the perfect energy to make it a reality. If you think your goal is something "nice to have," then there is a high probability that you won't get it. Your mind needs emotions to generate energy that triggers significant actions. A "nice to have " feeling is fragile in terms of the emotions it produces.

Take the three goals you feel you MUST have. There should be no room for doubt because you will commit to giving 100% of yourself until you reach them.

Now, look at your top priorities to determine if your top three goals conflict with any of your priorities. Some of your priorities may change as you move forward in your journey, which is perfectly ok. They should not be written in stone. Every time you set up a new goal, come back and cross-check it with your top priorities, and make sure to know what your highest priorities are so you don't compromise them at any point without your awareness and consent. For example, if your top priority is building a strong relationship with your children, having a goal that will demand an excessive number of hours away from them would be contradictory. Quality time and interaction are the number one requirement to build strong bonds. If you decide to move forward with activities in conflict with your top priorities, I suggest that you choose a time frame for this conflict to exist. Additionally, if you decide to take a job that requires 90% of traveling time, while your top priority is your family, make sure this conflict will exist for a short time frame and doesn't impede the time required to strengthen the bond with your family.

Conflicts between our goals and top core priorities can exist from time to time. As long as they are for a short period otherwise, they become the number one root cause for significant regrets.

About twelve years ago, I got a job offer with an excellent financial incentive that would have given me considerable extra income. This job had some responsibilities with sales and marketing. The new role required me to entertain clients at company events and dinners. This task, on its own, was the main reason I did not take the job. Why? Because it conflicted with one of my top priorities, which was having dinner with my family every night.

Similar to the last anecdote, a few years ago, I passed on a very generous financial opportunity that would have tripled my income in addition to a very lucrative bonus and other financial incentives. It was a tough decision to let this one go, but, again, it required me to be away from my kids for a considerable amount of time, and this conflict would have continued for many years.

In this case, I was not able to determine a definite time frame for this conflict. I chose to stand by my top priority, and even though it was a challenging decision at the time when I look back, it is rewarding to know how it proved to be the right one.

Understanding your goals and priorities and the relationship between them is critical in making the correct decisions that won't bring you regret in the future. Remember, you can buy many things but time is not one of them. Keeping your eye on your priorities ensures you invest and use your time on the things that matter most. You are the only one that can prioritize the happenings in your life. No one can feel the emotions triggered when you get into a conflicting situation that causes you to neglect your core values and priorities. Your top priorities can be different from the ones of your parents or your best friends. They are unique to you. Cross-checking your priorities with your goals will enable the right thoughts and emotions to make the correct choices. Once you make the first choice, similar opportunities will continue to come your way.

If you choose to pursue a goal, despite conflicting with your core priorities, make sure to define the time frame this conflict will exist. Naturally, your mind can get used to existing situations against your core values and priorities, mainly when the set of activities you engage in is so high that there is no time to reflect on current behaviors and choices.

Have you experienced a feeling that desires a change while you're taking time away from a current set of activities? Have you come up with ideas about re-inventing your life and building other financial incentives? If this happens to you, then take some time to understand the underlying causes of these desires. Many of these internal conflicts can be resolved by aligning your goals with your priorities.

If your goals and top three priorities are in complete conflict, you need to go back and either change your plan or assign a determined time frame for the conflict to exist. In addition, go back and review your priority list and double-check if your rankings are correct.

THE OΣU - LEVEL 5
DAILY EXERCISES -PURPOSE AND INTENTIONS

In Level 5, you will learn to use strategic intentions and techniques daily to build new habits that will become the foundation for attaining your objectives and goals. These daily practices build the infrastructure to obtain awareness and understanding with yourself and your subconscious mind. Balancing your mind with your actions will enable you to experience more satisfying and fulfilling results in everything you do.

To succeed in the OΣU, you must be aware of your daily activities. This is best achieved by building the habit of silence. Building the habit of silence and regularly setting up intentions will set your mind up for creativity, enjoyment, motivation, and energy. You can perform this routine at any time of the day. To get the most benefits, I encourage you to adopt this short routine first thing in the morning, right after waking up, and before getting out of bed while you are still a little sleepy. During this stage, your subconscious mind is more susceptible to suggestions. You can start utilizing five minutes as a starting point, and then you can increase by five more minutes at a time until you can quiet the mind for at least twenty minutes within a twenty-four-hour period.

You might think you are too busy with other stuff and lack time for this activity. Still, I highly suggest investing at least five minutes of your day in engaging in this morning exercise, where you combine silencing the mind with setting up intentions for the day. You can incorporate a couple of 2-5 minutes sessions at different times during the day to quiet your mind. The time you invest in silencing your mind will give you great dividends in your life, which can be measured on the quality and quantity of your outcome. You will begin to notice how your time is a lot more productive on the days you practice compared to days where you don't take the time to quiet your mind.

For this mini-version of factoring in some quiet time, be intentional and state it clearly; there's a message you send to yourself, your inner being, and your subconscious mind during the first thirty seconds or so. The intention can be something like "I can always find a solution." "Thank you for awareness of my potential and purpose." "Today, I will add value to everything I do." Or simply, "Thank you." Then quiet your mind.

I have discovered that one of the best ways for me to clear my head and enter into a mediation zone or daydreaming state is by closing my eyes and creating vivid images of being in a theater staring at the white or black huge screen. Paying attention to breathing is another effective way. Another method is by staring at the ceiling or any other point in the room. I find that looking at the flame of a candle is very peaceful and relaxing. If none of these techniques work for you, try listening to nature or meditation sounds or mantras. This method can be very effective when you need something specific to focus your attention on. After this exercise, at night, let yourself go to sleep with the certainty that the right answer will come to you.

If you have not done meditation in the past, it will take you some time to develop trust in this process. To start building this trust, make an intention related to a minor goal or simple target, something for which you can see results in a couple of days..

BENEFITS OF THIS MORNING ROUTINE:

» To quiet your mind at your will. This will minimize stress and enable the best decision-making.
» It will make your time more productive.
» It will energize your day with a positive set of emotions.
» It will plant the seed for constructive thoughts towards yourself and others.
» It will maximize your creativity and make you resourceful.
» It will trigger the initiative for forgiveness and gratitude.

Morning exercise routine, consists of four main actions

» Breathing – "baby breathing."
» Setting intentions- Including asking What and How
» Triggering Gratitude
» 15-30 minutes of physical exercise

While in a semi-sleep state, relax your jaw, inhale through your nose slowly, and let the air fill up your chest and stomach. This is similar to a baby's breathing. Afterward, open your mouth and let the air come out. Repeat this three times. At this point, your mind will be in an open state to receive your intentions. While the mind is in this calm state, think about a goal or purpose. Maintain an open mind with the expectancy that you will get what you are aiming for or better. Leaving the door open for something better opens the gateway for your subconscious mind to be creative. It also shows you new paths with choices you couldn't have asked for.

Once you have your mind in a peaceful state, keep your eyes closed, and imagine pulling down a movie screen where you see yourself performing an activity. Imagine that you have achieved your goal. Keep it simple. It should feel natural. If you are trying to build a solution or business, visualize yourself celebrating the achievement of the solution. If you are trying to obtain a degree or specific job, see yourself as if you've already attained it. Perhaps you can see yourself going out for dinner to celebrate or anything else that portrays your life after your accomplishment. Positive visualizations will trigger the positive emotions of achievement.

Now, set your intentions for the day, including asking

yourself "How?" and "What?" "What can I do to make something better, to add more value?" "How can I use the resources I have right now to head off in the right direction?" Be creative with your intentions to make it specific to your goals. Please don't try to resolve it at this point. Just set the intentions and quiet your mind for a few minutes.

If at any point during your morning routine, a negative thought or doubt comes to mind and triggers anger, sadness, or frustration, use any of the techniques previously discussed that can help you block the adverser chain of thoughts. Furthermore, you can incorporate any mantra that resonates with you to help block and dissipate these negative emotions.

To complete your morning exercise, sit up with your back straight, or you may continue lying down. Place our hands over your stomach so you can feel your stomach muscles moving. Start breathing in and out through your nose rapidly and forcefully. This exercise can make you feel dizzy if it's the first time you are doing it. Start by doing 1-3 cycles of 5-10 in-and-out rapid breaths. Some experts suggest doing this exercise by placing the tip of your tongue over the back of your front teeth. Others suggest touching the roof of your mouth with your tongue. I have done this both ways and noticed that it provides an energy boost as long as I kept my mouth closed, and my jaw relaxed. The main objective of this breathing exercise is to get you out of the sleepy stage and to send an energy boost to every part of your body and mind.

Finalize the exercise by allowing yourself to feel grateful for anything you value in your life and for the new great things to come. At this point, your mind will have everything it needs to give you the fuel and creativity required to make the most of your day.

Right after your breathing exercise, it's time to take care of your body by engaging in any physical activity for at least 15 ~ 30 minutes. Alternatively, an exercise routine is beneficial at any point that works for you during the day.

DAYTIME CHECKPOINTS

These daily checkpoints' objectives are to help maintain awareness and constructive thoughts, emotions, and actions. These checkpoints consist of the following:

- Feeding your mind.
- Remembering your intentions for the day.
- De-escalating situation through AIR ~ Act Instead of React.
- Exercising the OΣU three A's (Awareness, Actions, Accountability).
- Sharpen or get new knowledge in your area of expertise and interests required to achieve new goals.
- Supervising your T.E.A. cycle (Thoughts➔Emotions➔ Actions)

If you spend any time commuting, try to invest most of this time reading or listening to positive inspiration and motivational books, speeches, or podcasts. You can read or listen to anything that lifts your spirits. Feeding your mind with positive and constructive information will shield you from toxic energies that circulate among you. This practice is especially beneficial when you do it before starting your day. It will also better prepare you to deal with people who specialize in bringing negativism wherever they go. It will baseline for your mindset to deal with stressful situations constructively.

At any time during the day in which you face negative thoughts or arguments, you can block this chain of un-constructivism by using one or more of these methodologies:

- Go for a walk.
- Run images of the argument while picturing the person you're arguing with as a funny character or cartoon.
- Gain internal power and balance your mind through AIR (Acting Instead of Reacting)

AIR – Act Instead of React. Dealing with feelings of rage, disgust, anger, and frustration can be very tough for some people. This process requires controlling your emotions at the moment while dealing with arguments, criticism, and situations where you may feel aggression directly towards yourself. Independent of the facts or emotional perceptions that caused these types of feelings, the reality is that you are experiencing the strong negative and unconstructive emotions, and they need to be controlled. Anyone can keep their composure when things are going their way, but being able to control and manage troubling emotions in the middle of a heated situation is an art. The best-case scenario is to stop the argument or awkward situation from escalating. Suppose this is an argument you need to address. In that case, this technique - AIR - will enable us to lower the internal heat to a level where we can communicate our opinions without overloading emotions. One exercise to deescalate the situation is to run the argument in your mind while replacing the main character with something hilarious: a cartoon character or a funny superhero. While trying to create these images, your mind will find it difficult to achieve. This is similar to doing math problems to help during a panic attack. The idea is to make your mind struggle to try to put these images together, which helps to shift your thoughts from your negative thoughts. Most thoughts generating the emotions that trigger adverse reactions will get blocked. By the time you've finished the exercise of replacing the image in your mind, your level of negative emotions will be manageable enough for you to make the most suitable decisions about what your next course of action should be.

- The last step in the daily routine is to dedicate some time to learning and sharpening your line of work or business skills that align with your primary goals.

NIGHTLY EXERCISE ROUTINE.

This exercise has the most benefits when executing before going to bed. This exercise can also be incorporated for anyone who has a night job; you'll simply follow the guidelines before you sleep schedule.

THE 4-7-8 BREATHING TECHNIQUE

The 4-7-8 Breathing Technique -Start by exhaling all air from your lungs, making an 'Ahhhhh' sound. Then inhale and count 1 to 4 in your mind while keeping your mouth closed. Hold this breath while counting from 1 to 7. Finally, open your mouth and exhale while counting from 1 to 8 and make the 'Ahhhhh' sound—repeat this cycle three times.

By now, your mind should be clear to focus on anything you want to get an answer for whether you're looking for a solution to a problem at work or with someone. Or perhaps you needed clarity related to one of your goals. You've opened your mind to more clear focus. So, spend one to two minutes visualizing your solutions to the issue you are trying to solve. However, I don't want you to try and come up with a solution just yet. Let things marinate, and a clear answer will manifest the following day(s) or in the middle of the night. I like to keep a pen and paper next to my bed to write any idea that comes to me in the middle of the night. Otherwise, it is very likely I won't remember it in the morning. If this is the first time you are doing this type of problem-solving technique, it may take you a little longer for the answers to come to your conscious mind.

Finish the evening routine by setting intentions like, "Tomorrow will be a great day!" "Everything is thriving for the better." "I can always find a solution." Be creative and make intentions that are important for you.

THE ZERO-SUM GAME OF YOU
CHEAT SHEET

The OΣU Highlight	Leader in You	Hopeless in You
Morning Routine Breathing techniques - "baby breathing" and intentions for the day, including Adding value to something	The winner takes 1 point	The winner takes 1 point
Morning Routine Motivation and learning something - listening to at least one motivational quote, speech, or self-development book.	The winner takes 1 point	The winner takes 1 point
Practicing 3 A's concerning your targets	The winner takes 1 point	The winner takes 1 point
Supervising AIR	The winner takes 1 point	The winner takes 1 point
Supervising TEA		
At least one action related to your targets	The winner takes 1 point	The winner takes 1 point
At least 15-30 minutes of physical exercise	The winner takes 1 point	The winner takes 1 point
Evening Routine Reviewing day status & breathing technique -4-7-8	The winner takes 1 point	The winner takes 1 point
Evening Routine Setting questions and intentions for tomorrow	The winner takes 1 point	The winner takes 1 point

The Protector. This is a bonus point. Any act of compassion or kindness that helps in any way or brightens someone's day (outside immediate inner circle). You can use this point against a loss to the hopeless side in you, in addition, it will start generating the intangible of gratitude and fulfillment.

THE ZERO-SUM GAME OF
YOUR LOVED ONES

Have you ever wished to get into a loved one's mind to understand why they behave in a certain way or why they don't take action about what seems so apparent as the right course of action? This loved one can be your parent, child, partner, friend, or someone very close to you. Trying to put yourself in someone else's shoes is not as easy as it sounds. It isn't practical in most cases. This is because even if we put ourselves in the other person's shoes, we will see reality through our custom lenses. It's simple; no one can live or experience another person's life because one fact will be experienced as a different reality, which will trigger thoughts and emotions according to that specific individual. Understanding this reality and keeping an open mind to support your loved ones without making judgments based on your expectations is the best help you can give them to find their path to happiness.

We all want to see the ones we love happy, satisfied, and successful. We want them to be proud of who they are. We often want to protect them from pain and struggles based on our own experience. Here is the thing, just like we are responsible and accountable for our game, they also have a game to play. The only way for them to grow is by living their own experiences, understanding their thoughts and emotions, and learning how to use them for their benefit.

It is possible we've walked along a rocky path and hurt our toes multiple times, sort of speak. Hence, we want to stop our loved ones from going the same way. Depending on where they are mentally and emotionally, they may listen to us and change their path. But in other cases, if they are not ready, we will have to let them figure it out for themselves. Our loved ones have a mind of their own, and they must face their unique challenge so that their attitude and character will be strengthened. We can have the best intentions to help them avoid future pain or discouragement or to ensure that they don't make the same mistakes we did, but despite our good intentions, the fact is, we need to let them grow by overcoming their challenges. They need space to expand their wings, even if those wings lead them in a completely different direction than where we'd like to see them.

Our loved ones, just like each one of us, will be attracted to encounters related to their own game. We can make them aware of our experiences, thoughts, and guidance while understanding their growth needs.

When I was younger, I thought that when two people were in love, one could make the other change because of love. I learned later that it was a fallacy. A person can only change when they perceive those changes as something they want to make. Sometimes, people change just to make others happy;

they may compromise their core interests and values to be more likable by their peers. We may influence someone for a while, like boyfriends and girlfriends who often engage in activities despite their interest, only to be next to the person they feel love and passion for. However, as the relationship advances and commitments are made, the individual's core priorities, interests, and goals will surface or resurface. Once that happens, it can trigger a series of arguments and complaints become daily life.

Children are more like a "sponge," susceptible to absorbing a lot of information from their environment and those surrounding them. During their early years, parents or guardians have the responsibility to help them construct their core foundation. What they are taught and how the behaviors they see by their caregivers will significantly impact their lives and who they become. We raise our children and teach them our point of view, but this does not mean they have to follow it. As they grow older, they will have their interests and may begin to see things differently than we do.

There is a saying that "every generation thinks they are smarter than the prior and wiser than the next." There is some truth to this. Most likely, we think we are smarter than our parents; this could be because of technology, higher education, or just because we were born in a different era. Similarly, we may believe that we know better than our kids because we are older and wiser. Even after kids reach adulthood, it is very likely for parents to think they are still wiser. Regardless of where we stand, our children, parents, family members, and friends will attract their own unique experiences according to the game they decide to play.

Each of our loved ones has their own unique set of talents, which can make them successful. We can guide and teach them the importance of believing in themselves and being persistent with their goals, but we need to let them go and have their own experiences. They will be responsible and accountable for their actions, just like we are of ours. Forcing someone to change against their will is impossible. If a friend constantly makes excuses for everything or engages in activities, we do not support them. We can strive to help for a while. But if, after multiple attempts, they continue to go on a path we disagree with, we can decide to stay away from them or recognize and accept them the way they are. Keep in mind that the ones we spend the most time with will influence our life one way or another.

If we feel we cannot be ourselves with our parents or grandparents or resent those who raised us, understand that a parent wants the best for a child in most cases and with some exceptions. The root of the problem may lie in how they were raised and the access to information and education they had at hand. Also, they have their list of habits and beliefs that can sometimes hurt them as well. If you identify with this scenario, the best way to overcome these feelings is by opening your mind and heart to see the overall picture that might influence their lives [and yours]. Feeling compassion and kindness will free you from those negative emotions of the past. You receive the key to opening many doors to gratitude, happiness, and fulfillment when that happens.

Not everyone is aware of their own game; each person's

mind works differently. We all have different habits, cultures, education, beliefs, and environments that have affected our existing behaviors. We can help our loved ones by being understanding, caring, and loving, as their personalities and characters grow at their own pace and through their own experiences.

DEALING WITH
UNPREVENTABLE EVENTS

Painful emotions will manifest as a result of losing someone dear to you and are usually tough to manage. It hurts, even more, when the pain results in events beyond your control. In such cases, you will need time and space to deal with the loss. Trying to ignore or cover up such emotions will only delay the healing process. There are different ways to deal with emotions that result from tragic events. The guidelines of the OΣU will help you cope constructively. It will not change the circumstances, but it will help you react, handle, and assimilate the events more constructively while minimizing the elapse of the time you're in deep pain.

I decided to write a segment about the loss of a loved one, based on my experience from many years ago. However, three months after I wrote the segment, my family and I went through the tragic event of losing one more member of our immediate inner family. This time it was my dearest sister, Maria Isabel. She used to introduce me to her friends as "mi hermanita" (my little sister). We had a very special relationship. When I first heard this unexpected news on a bright, beautiful Saturday morning, it felt like everything stopped. I was in denial. My denial was then followed by an overwhelming heavy pain that sucked my breath away, over and over, like a fish gasping for air.

Sympathy cards in a department store have words like "heavy heart" as part of the message. I had seen such cards before, but I never understood what that meant until I lost my sister. A heavy heart means that your heart feels "heavy;" it feels like it is dragging you down underwater, and you cannot float out. Until that moment, I didn't know what that truly felt like. If you have lost a dear loved one, you know how heavy it feels within your chest and the weakness in your mind and soul. That weakness makes it more challenging to hold on to what can brighten your days. One loss does not prepare us for another. The loss of a loved one is the most harrowing emotional experience I believe a person can feel. It hurts afresh whenever we remember our loved one as we go through the healing process. But there is hope. Like my oldest brother, Juan Lopez, would encourage us the day after my sister passed, "Every day, families are dealing with the pain of losing a loved one. Every day, in all countries all over the world, there is someone in pain because of the passing of a loved one; it just happens that today it is our time."

If you are experiencing something similar, don't despair, it will get better. I promise you. If you are dealing with something like this, you are not alone. Your heart will feel heavy and shattered for some time, and you may feel you can't get out of bed or engage in any activities without feeling pain. I can assure you, regardless of how bad it is, it will get better.

Every exercise or training program starts with a

minimum amount of effort. In the case of weightlifting, maybe a trainee begins by lifting two or five pounds. As they get stronger, they will start to lift heavier weights. This way, little by little, they can build the muscles to become strong enough to sustain a fifty or one-hundred-pound weights. It does not happen automatically on the first attempt. Dealing with the loss of a loved one is like having to lift a five-hundred-pound weight when we are only prepared to lift five or ten pounds. It is overwhelming, painful, and sometimes devastating. The strength of these hurtful feelings will diminish, and you will be able to change these saddening emotions into a celebration of their life. I believe that when I leave this earth, I will like to see my loved ones moving on without pain. Our dearly departed have these same thoughts; they would love to see us moving on and finding happiness. They live in us, and what we do with our life is a reflection of their life's impact on ours.

If those you hold dear are still with you, you are in the best position to show them love and care, NOW. Don't miss this opportunity. You don't know when it will be the last time you will get to see them. This is the rule about living without regrets. If you are kind, loving, and show care to the ones you love, when that painful moment comes, you will know in your heart that every encounter with that person was lived to the fullest. You will feel satisfied that you enjoyed and valued them while they were alive. Caring and showing love to your loved ones ensures there will be no void in your heart when they depart. You won't have the desire to reverse time because of regrets. So, if you can still hold the person, you love and tell them how much you love them, then do it. Actions speak louder than words; that's why showing your loved ones how much they mean to you is important.

You are building your history today. Be sure your loved ones know how much they mean to you and give them the attention they need according to the phase of life you all are in. Managing your priorities and balancing your life will enable you to enjoy the present. Yes, make plans for the future, but don't forget about living your life today, to the fullest.

Dealing with unexpected sickness, living during a dictatorship, a war, or a pandemic are all unforeseen events that can wreck your mental state and relationships. Under these circumstances, the same rules apply. Maintaining your awareness to manage your thoughts and emotions will enable you to act instead of reacting, hence making the most of what you have around you, efficiently overcoming these circumstances, and creating your best possible outcome

THE OΣU WRAPPER
BALANCE OF HUMANITY

The French philosopher Voltaire-Francois-Marie Arouet – (1694 -1778) said, "Words like luck, chance and coincidence were invented to express the known effects of the unknown causes." You are not alone in this world. What you do will affect someone else somehow, and sooner or later, each action you take will bring you a reaction. You can see this as collecting what is sown.

The OΣU emphasizes that you have complete control of your lives and are accountable for your results. It also makes you aware of pursuing goals without having regrets as part of your success. The end does not justify the means. The guidance on this game is intertwined with a more central principle: what you do will somehow affect someone else, and all of your actions will bring back a reaction. The same goes the other way around. You are affected in one way or another by others' behavior, decisions, and actions—many call it the law of cause and effect. According to Ralph Waldo Emerson, you get back what you put out. He continues by saying that "cause and effect are two sides of one fact."

If you believe that there is karma, you may behave very differently from someone that doesn't. Believing in karma is not better than not believing in it, as long as your actions don't negatively affect someone else. We are all somehow connected in some way. Every action will trigger a reaction, and our collective actions affect generations to come. The environmental, social, and political issues we face today are the combined outcomes from prior generations' actions and inaction, combined with our actions and inactions.

We have an incredible opportunity to make a difference for ourselves and our descendants. Be a believer, a doer, a go-getter. Become the happiest and fulfilled version of yourself. Go ahead and play your game with pride and celebrate who you are. Show the world what you have to offer, embrace the strength you have in you. You are the only person who can be YOU. That is an incredible gift, and it is up to you to grow to your full potential. If you focus on playing the $O\Sigma U$ successfully, not only will you achieve a life of abundance, awareness, and fulfillment, you will also contribute to the bigger game that we all are part of. Future generations will be thankful for the actions you are taking today. You'll make the very best of your present and build a brighter future for yourself, your loved ones, and humanity.

As individuals, we are all part of our home ecosystem and the county and city ecosystems. All these sectors are part of the state which is part of a country. All countries are part of the world's ecosystem. The world is thus part of the Universe's ecosystem. Each ecosystem needs a balance to perform at its best. If there are constant arguments and fights in your house, the energy flow will be out of balance due to this continuous bickering. These arguments will make it challenging for all the ecosystem members to succeed while in that environment. Just like if there are many break-ins and robberies in your area, these events will affect how people behave in your neighborhood. And if our country is battling a war, dealing with terror attacks, or has significant financial and educational differences, the country's ecosystem will be unstable.

The way your actions affect others' lives will eventually change your own or your loved ones' lives. You can take this as karma or the process of cause and effect. But the fact is, there are more opportunities for everyone in a society that has more available resources. The world is a living organism, just like our body. If our body gets any critical sickness in one leg, stomach, or any other part of the body, the whole body will work as one to battle the illness. The cells that make our bones or brain cannot say, "Hey, you, cells from the stomach, this is your problem to resolve." All of the organs will die if the illness is kept unattended.

What we do in one part of our ecosystem will have effects on another. That is the bigger game that we all are components of. Many times, some events affect an entire society, country, or even the entire world. The combined results from all players' games will result in creating a mixed reaction. This significantly impacts the overall balance of the world as a whole and future generations.

You are unique and have a set of talents that have a role to play in this bigger game to keep the ecosystem in balance. From the End-Game perspective, the strength comes from the balance of all the players. The success of this game will be the outcome of your collective consciousness, where you gain awareness of how your thoughts, emotions, and actions affect others.

You are the only one accountable for your outcome. Define your priorities, set your targets, and play your game with a purpose. Everyone can contribute something to help the overall balance of humankind. By taking full ownership of your game and understanding how these outcomes affect other people's games, you will contribute to humanity's total stability, so the higher ecosystem does not have to correct itself.

BIBLIOGRAPHY

Christakis, N. A. (2008/05/22). The Collective Dynamics of Smoking in a Large Social Network: NEJM. New England Journal of Medicine.

Sanders, R. (1987). THE PARETO PRINCIPLE: ITS USE AND ABUSE. Journal of Services Marketing, 1(2), 37-40. Retrieved 6 4, 2020, from https://emerald.com/insight/content/doi/10.1108/eb024706/full/html

ROSA L. ANTONINI

A devoted philanthropist and Software Engineer. Throughout the years, she noticed the similarities between human behaviors and software engineering. She is deeply passionate about helping others open their minds and hearts to live a life of self-fulfillment. Her debut book, *The Zero-Sum Game of You,* came to her as an inspiration born from her sense of gratitude.

Since her early upbringing, Rosa has been fascinated with learning about science and metaphysics. This pursuit of interests influenced the core foundation of her values and sensitivity to others. Rosa has always been empathetic and compassionate with a strong desire to identify ways to help decrease others' suffering.

In *The Zero-Sum Game of You*, Rosa compares how the human mind and body functions under its own set of codes, just like computer software, except that computer software coding is somewhat permanent. Still, humans have the divine opportunity and control to recode their way of thinking and behaving. She believes this transformation can happen if an individual is willing to adopt and adapt to a new way of thinking, which drives a new way of behaving; ultimately improving their lives and relationships. Rosa has developed a 63-day "game of life," which she represents as a zero-sum game that focuses on relinquishing negative habits and building new positive and sustainable habits.

Rosa is very aware of the difficulties and challenges one must go through when there is nothing more than a desire or an idea. Because of this, 60% of her book's funds will be dedicated to creating training and educational programs to help others achieve better and more fulfilling jobs.

Visit her website at www.rosaantonini.com

CPSIA information can be obtained
at www.ICGtesting.com
Printed in the USA
BVHW011258220322
632097BV00002B/4